AYATULLAH IBRAHIM AMINI

Principles of the Shi'ite Creed

First published by ABWA Publishing and Printing Center 2012

Copyright © 2012 by Ayatullah Ibrahim Amini

All rights reserved. No part of this publication may be reproduced, stored or transmitted in any form or by any means, electronic, mechanical, photocopying, recording, scanning, or otherwise without written permission from the publisher. It is illegal to copy this book, post it to a website, or distribute it by any other means without permission.

First edition

Translation by Ali Reza'i

Contents

Foreword	1
Translator's Note	4
Introduction	6
Imitation In The Secondary Principles Of The Religion	8
The Life of Ants	14
Remarks by Imam as-Sadiq ('a)	16
God Is Wise, Capable And Living	18
God is All-Hearing and All-Seeing	20
The First Argument	22
The Second Reason for the Unity of God	25
The Necessity of the Appointments Of Prophets	30
Man is Social	32
Prophets Must Perform Miracles	35
The Qur'an, the Immortal Miracle	37
Who Has Been Appointed as the successor of the Prophet?	45
The Prophetic Mission And The Leadership Of Imams Are...	46
The Hadith of Ghadir	48
Hadith al-Thaqalayn	49
The Hadith of Jabir	50
The Relationship Between The Divine Justice And Wisdom And...	53
The Resurrection is Corporeal	56
The Implications of the Faith in the Resurrection	57

The Great Prophet's Conduct	60
'Ali's Will	64
The Woman Who Introduced 'Ali to Mu'awiyah	65
Some Remarks by Imam al-Hasan	69
Imam Hasan's Peace Agreement	70
The Text of the Peace Agreement	73
A Lesson From The School of Imam Husayn	76
Excerpts From Imam Husayn's Supplications	78
Some Remarks by Imam al-Sajjad	80
Some Remarks by Imam Baqir	82
His Advice On Deathbed	84
Some Remarks by the Imam (Part One)	86
Some Remarks by the Imam (Part Two)	88
Some Remarks by the Imam (Part Three)	91
Some Remarks by the Imam (Part Four)	93
Some Remarks by the Imam (Part Five)	96
Peoples' Duties During The Occultation	99
Is It Possible That Someone Might Live Over 1000 Years?	100

Foreword

In the Name of Allah, the All-Beneficent, the All-Merciful

The precious legacy left behind by the Holy Prophet's Household [*ahl al-bayt*] (may peace be upon them all) and their followers' preservation of this legacy from the menace of extinction is a perfect example of an all-encompassing school [*maktab*], which embraces the different branches of Islamic knowledge.

This school has been able to train many talented personalities by quenching them with this gushing fountain. This school has presented scholars to the Muslim *ummah* who, by following the Holy Prophet's Household ('a), have occupied the station of clarifying doubts and skepticisms brought forth by various creeds and intellectual currents both inside and outside Muslim society. Throughout the past centuries, they have presented the rmest answers and solutions to these doubts.

Anchored in the responsibilities it is shouldering, the Ahl al-Bayt ('a) World Assembly has embarked upon defending the sanctity of *risalah* [messengership] and its authentic beliefs—truths which have always been opposed by the chiefs and leaders of anti-Islamic sects, religions and trends. In this sacred path, the Assembly regards itself as a follower of the upright pupils of the school of the Ahl al-Bayt ('a)—those who have always been ready to refute those accusations and calumnies and have tried to be always in the frontline of this struggle on the basis of the expediencies of time and space.

The experiences in this eld, which have been preserved in the books of scholars belonging to the school of the Ahl al-Bayt ('a), are unique in their own right. It is because these experiences have been based upon knowledge ['ilm] and the preeminence of the intellect and reasoning, and at the same time, they are completely devoid of blind prejudice, whim and caprice. These experiences address experts, scholars and thinkers in a manner that is acceptable to a healthy mind and the pure human natural disposition [trah].

In a bid to assist those who are in quest of truth, the Ahl al-Bayt ('a) World Assembly has endeavored to enter a new phase of these worthy experiences within the framework of research and translating the works of contemporary Shi'ah writers or those who, through divine guidance, have embraced this noble school.

The Assembly is also engaged in the study and publication of the valuable works of pious predecessors and outstanding Shi'ah personalities so that those who are thirsty for the truth could quench their thirst from this refreshing fountain by listening and embracing this truth, which the Holy Prophet's Household ('a) has offered as a gift to the entire world.

It is hoped that our dear readers would not deprive the Ahl al-Bayt ('a) World Assembly of their valuable opinions, suggestions and constructive criticisms in this arena.

We also invite scholars, translators and other institutions to assist us in propagating the pure Muhammadan (S) Islam.

We ask God, the Exalted, to accept this trivial effort and enhance it further under the auspices of His vicegerent on earth, Hadrat al-Mahdi (may Allah, the Exalted, expedite his glorious advent).

It is appropriate here to express our utmost gratitude to Ayatollah Shaykh Ibrahim Amini for writing the book, and to Mr. Ali Reza'i for translating it, as well as to all our honorable colleagues in accomplishing this task especially the dear ones in the Translation Ofce for undertaking this responsibility.

Cultural Affairs Department
The Ahl al-Bayt ('a) World Assembly

Translator's Note

Our actions and our conduct are the results of our beliefs. A faithful person, believing in God and the Day of Resurrection, leads a completely different life from that of a non-believer. A set of moral and human virtues constitute the foundations of the believer's life, because he considers death as the opening to another world and believes that death is not tantamount to dissolution of his life and therefore in the hope of reward or out of fear of the Judgment Day, avoids wrongdoing and evil deeds, volunteers for useful activities, whereas a non-believer's situation is at the opposite end of the pole.

Therefore, those who seek felicity and prosperity for their society should promote faith among individuals because an individual's felicity is not separate from that of the society.

About twenty years ago, a group of Iranian expatriates asked the honorable jurisprudent Ayatullah Subhani to compile a brief and concise article about the primary principles of the Islamic beliefs to familiarize themselves and their acquaintances with them.

He composed an article which was subsequently sent and welcomed by them and later on it was translated and published in other languages. After a while, a number of friends noted that if a compelling but simple book on the primary principles of the religion was published, it would prove useful to religious gatherings and high schools.

To achieve this objective, the honorable master called on me to compile a book by supplementing that article. In obedience to his request, all the sections of that article were rewritten elaborately and extensively, and the book was published. From then onward, tens of thousands of copies of the book have been published by *Dar al-Fikr* publications and have been utilized across the country.

Recently, having decided to reprint the book, the publications has made slight corrections that is hoped to render it more useful.

Reza Ostadi, Qum Seminary

Introduction

The primary principles of the religion are a series of beliefs (unity, justice, the prophetic mission, the leadership of Imams, and the Resurrection) which constitute the foundations of the faith. Since there have been various beliefs that have prevailed in the human communities, or in other words, each group has propagated its own peculiar set of beliefs, therefore it is incumbent upon everyone to identify the primary principles of their faith through reasoning, so they could withstand the toxic propaganda of their prejudiced opponents and not be diverted every day.

Of course when it is said that everyone should learn the primary principles of his faith through reasoning it does not mean that each person should engage in a prolonged study of religion and should extensively study philosophical and argumentative books but he should do so to the extent that he could know the foundations of his faith with solid but simple reasons. It is helpful to recall the story of an old woman busy spinning, who was asked,

"What reasons do you have to establish the existence of God?"

She stopped working immediately and as the wheel came to a standstill, said,

Introduction

"While such a little wheel needs a person to spin it, how could one say that the immense world with all the awe-inspiring heavenly bodies that revolve, have spun on their own or without an operator?"

Imitation In The Secondary Principles Of The Religion

Having learned the foundations of his faith through reection and sound reasoning, one can imitate a qualied jurisprudent who is an expert in deducing divine edicts from its sources in the secondary principles such as questions about prayers, fasting, Hajj pilgrimage, and transactions and so on and so forth. Here imitation signies consulting the experts. Just as in our lives, when we don't know anything well, we seek experts in those areas, for instance, when we fall ill, we see a doctor or when we want to build a house, we seek an architect, similarly, in the secondary principles and beliefs and divine commands, if the person is not an expert, that is, a jurisprudent, he should consult a qualied jurisprudent and follow his opinions and insights.

Having ended the childhood and attained a discrimination between good and evil, if one consults his conscience, he will realize that he inherently loves virtues such as honesty, justness, and sympathy, that is, he appreciates the goodness of these traits and for this recognition he does not need any instruction or book, and if he is asked,

"How did you understand that honesty is a virtue?"

He would reply, "I did not learn this through reasoning but the recognition of its goodness is mingled with my conscience and nature."

The belief in the existence of God (the Creator of the universe and its inhabitants) rests parallel to such inherent beliefs and to obtain this belief one does not need to be instructed or educated, but rather by consulting his nature and conscience, he will realize that this universe possesses an Omniscient and Omnipotent Creator.

Therefore, when we look back on the past history of mankind, we see that the belief in the existence of God has existed through all the previous eras even among people who lived in a savage manner and were not acquainted with culture and education. Of course, they occasionally erred in identifying God and assumed that sun or some stars or some earthly creatures are the creator of the universe but they never did without a principal belief in the existence of God.

Having claried the meaning of an inherent belief in the existence of God, we should bear in mind one point:

At times, inherent things are neglected due to certain causes. Just as a light covered by a thick cloth which will stop illuminating, the God-knowing nature is occasionally covered by thick curtains of negligence, scientic conceit or over-indulgence in instinctive and impulsive desires. In this case, it is as if there were no such faith (in the existence of God) in one's nature. But when these curtains are removed, one will automatically return to God.

Those who have deviated from the authentically innate belief in God as a result of wrongdoing and indulgence in instinctual desires will return to God and seek His help whenever they confront danger and feel that they can't escape the threat by seeking ordinary means, for example, when they are faced with the threat of a plane crash or a car accident and so on. It demonstrates that at these moments, their God-knowing nature correctly manifests itself.

The sixth infallible Imam has concisely raised this point. Someone asked him to direct him toward the Creator of the universe (state reasons for His existence), the revered Imam replied thus,

"Have you ever been aboard a ship?" "Yes."

"Has it ever happened that you have had a shipwreck and there was no other ship to rescue you and you didn't know how to reach safety? (You could not rescue yourself through ordinary means).

"Yes."

"When you were desperately hopeless, did not you turn, deep in your soul, to one that would be able to save you?"

"Yes, I felt that there is a power which can save me."

Imam al-Sadiq ('a) observed, "The power toward whom you turned is God."[1]

This demonstrates that the power toward which the stricken people turn, intentionally or otherwise, and the same power to which one returns after removing the curtains of haughtiness, egoism, reliance on other people and dependence on supercial means, is the Creator of the universe who can fulll needs and rescue the aficted.

If you consider a watch or a sewing machine or a refrigerator, a motorcycle, a car or an airplane, you will discover a peculiar order in each of them. Do you think it is probable that these precise and neat systems could have arisen on their own and without the involvement of scientists and thinkers?

If you don't regard this logical that the engine of an airplane with its awesome order and sophistication could have come on its own, then how about the amazing systems operating throughout the world whose every corner is thousand times as exact and precise as the engine of a plane or car. How was it created?

What is the source of the astonishing order and the hidden secrets of the creatures of the world that are so mysterious that they have

---

[1] Al-Tawhid by al-Saduq, new print, p. 231.

bewildered the thinkers?

With a little reection, man's wisdom and reason will conclude that an Omniscient and Omnipotent Creator has created this orderly world and its manifold creatures.

To appreciate the existence of order in the universe, it sufces to take one part of your body, for instance, your eyes into consideration.

This tiny system, that is, the eye is so precise and sophisticated that even the expert ophthalmologists who have spent years in studying it, are eventually forced to acknowledge their inability to solve all its secrets.

Can any reasonable individual consider it possible that eyes with their astonishing features and their precise structure could have come into existence on their own? The respiratory and digestive systems and other parts of the human body that are created according to special principles and rules do testify to the existence of a wise and capable Creator who has based all these on certain calculations and measurements.

Apart from man and his body, take a seed of wheat or a kernel of almond which emerge from the soil and turn into an ear of wheat or a fruitful tree. Since the seed is planted in the earth and penetrated the soil and emerges from the ground to grow into a shrub or a tree, what extensive and precise systems should be at work until that seed of wheat or that kernel of almond has completed it process. In fact, all these vast and amazing systems like the yearly seasons, days and nights and so on should cooperate like kind nurses so that a shrub or a tree ourishes and we could use their fruits.

Are not the almond tree and the shrub of wheat sufcient evidence to establish the existence of God and His Omnipotence and His Wisdom and Will? Could it be claimed that this order has arisen on its own?

Does man's reason let him think that sun, moon, stars, seasons, days and nights, and so on, have emerged on their own and does not have any creator? Mufadhdhal (one of Imam as-Sadiq's disciples) told him,

"When we explain the order of the universe, some materialists who are dubious about the existence of God or deny it, say, 'all these have been created by nature.'"

Imam al-Sadiq ('a) observed,

"If by nature, they mean something that has wisdom, capability and will and freedom, it's the same as God. They have given it the wrong name (because they have called God, the nature). If by nature, they mean something that does not have power and wisdom, this is out of the question, because it is not possible that such a neat and wonderful world could have been created by a blind and deaf and senseless nature."[2]

In short, given the conclusions of reason and reection, the universe possesses a wise and capable Creator who is "God" and it is impossible that an ignorant and senseless nature could have created such a precise system.

Again we return to the question of the creation of man. A person by himself is an immense world. Each part of his body attests to the boundless wisdom and capability of its Creator. And as the human knowledge is expanded and more secrets of the creation are disclosed, the existence of a powerful and wise Creator gets more obvious.

As we can see, a light from the Unseen is placed in everyone's nature, which guides him toward virtues, and felicity. This shining light is the faculty of *thought*.

Every new invention is the fruit of this power of "thought." All the books, libraries, and scientic majors have emerged due to the tremendous power of "thought." And this is the power of thought and reection that guides us toward felicity and prosperity, when we are faced with dilemmas. Who has endowed human beings with such a useful and wonderful power?

Could it be supposed that anyone but a wise Creator has bestowed

---

[2] Indirect quotation from Tawhid Mufadhdhal, Najaf, p.55.

such a great asset upon human beings? In the human body, a delicate, small, and precise system which weighs very little and has a delicate substance is placed. This system is called "brain," or the nervous center one of whose miraculous wonders is that it works completely on its own.

Human made calculators operate according to directions. They work as they are directed. But this automatic machine (brain or the nervous center) is just the opposite of these machines. Not only no direction is necessary, but it issues commands to the body and directs it.

The body itself is a machine that transforms substance into energy, but it is utterly different from human- made machines with similar function. Because such machines could only change special things into energy but the human body draws its raw materials from nature and transforms them into a variety of energies. Human body is endowed with automatic and advanced labs and drug companies in the form of "glands" each one of which is in charge of producing a certain substance, which performs a special duty of the different vital functions of the body.

Does not the existence of such orderly and exact machine testify to the creation of man by a wise and capable Creator?

The Life of Ants

Let's abandon man to take a look at the life of ant, this mysterious insect whose whole life teaches us the knowledge of God and His unity.

These tiny insects have founded their lives upon distribution of efforts, and close cooperation and perform tasks through understanding and contribution to one another. All of us have observed this close cooperation when they build a house or carry a burden.

This insect knows instinctively and through its God-given intelligence, without going to college or majoring in agriculture, that in order to prevent the decay of seeds, they should be divided in two and actually does this. If it notices that the seed is damp, it will take out the wet seed to expose it to sunlight and dry it. Furthermore, it constructs its house at a high altitude to keep it from being immersed in water.

Could it be said that it performs such amazing things without guidance from a higher authority? Who is the instructor of this little insect? From where it has learned such important lessons, and has founded its life upon them, that human could not have acquired unless they studied or learned through experience?[3]

---

[3] Abridged from Tawhid Mufadhdhal, Najaf, p.111.

Remarks by Imam as-Sadiq (a)

Abu Shakir Deisan, who was one of the materialists, called on the revered Imam, "Prove the existence of God for me!" he said.

As he posed this question, a boy was playing with an egg nearby. The revered Imam took the egg from the boy and turned to Abu Shakir and said,

"Do you see this egg? It has a fortress which is strong and rm. Inside this fortress, and beneath its walls, rests a thin layer and there are melted gold and silver inside it (the yellow and white uids of the egg). But these two parts are never mixed [could it be said that these two parts with this special quality could have come into being on their own?].

"Abu Shakir, no one knows whether the chicken that is hatched from this egg, will be male or female.

And when the chicken emerges from the egg, it has beautiful colors. (For example, consider the colorful feathers of the peacock. What power has so beautifully painted the chicken?). Is painting a chicken or a peacock less important that painting a picture? Could it be ever said that these paintings have painters but these natural colorings have arisen by themselves?

Then, he said to Abu Shakir, "Don't you agree that this egg and the chicken that is going to emerge from it with its attributes must have a thoughtful and wise Creator?"

Abu Shakir thought for a while as if he had been asleep and were suddenly awakened, and then he said, "Yes, I testify that the universe has a creator called "Allah" who possesses all the great qualities and testify that Muhammad is God's servant and His prophet and you are the Prophet's successor and God's proof on earth, obedience to whom is obligatory."[4]

Yes, any creature of this world, any atom or cell from the animate cells of creatures, testify to the existence of its Maker and Creator.

Any quality that bestows dignity and grandeur to its owner and eliminates deciency or shortcoming from him is called a great quality. For instance, take knowledge and enlightenment which remove ignorance from its owner and wipe out this shortcoming in him. Similarly, someone who is not strong and powerful is incomplete and the quality of strength or power will eliminate his defects.

The Creator of the world possesses all the great qualities and is free from shortcomings and defects. Because God is the one that fullls the needs of the world and bestows all the blessings and benets, therefore He should possess all the great qualities. It could never be assumed that one who does not possess a great quality could bestow it upon someone else. For instance, an illiterate person cannot do away with another's illiteracy. Now, read this argument in a more extended way.

---

[4] From Al-Ihtijaj by Tabarsi, Najaf, vol. 2, p. 71 and the same book, pp.181, 1350.

God Is Wise, Capable And Living

We could appreciate God's qualities by examining the creatures He has created. Because the vast universe whose every part has been created with precision and order and whose every creature has been fashioned with special features and certain calculations, is the strongest evidence that its Creator possesses knowledge, competence and power. The astonishing order of the universe (some of instances were studied in the preceding lessons) attests to the fact that its Creator is aware of every creature's secrets as well as the causes of their survival or destruction.

Every creature has been created with all-out knowledge and perfect deliberation. Having realized the qualities of knowledge and power in God, we can appreciate another quality of His, that is, life or the quality of being alive, because knowledge and power presuppose life. Anyone who enjoys knowledge and power must be alive.

God, the Exalted, has adorned Himself with every great quality (including knowledge, power and life) in His scripture [Qur'an]. Furthermore, He has introduced Himself as free from and innocent of any blemish or shortcoming.

"God is aware of everything" (The Holy Quran, Surah al-Baqara 2: 231).

"Indeed, God has power over everything" (The Holy Quran, Surah al-Baqarah 2: 148).

"He (God) is alive, and there is no god save Him. (The Holy Quran, Surah Ghar 40: 65).

Of course, as it was stated earlier, the universe with all its wonders and riddles clearly proves the knowledge, competence and life of its Creator. But the state of these qualities is not clear to us, because our thought and wisdom are limited and cannot have access to the true essence of the qualities of God. Indeed, no thought, however, high it might soar, can y over this tall and boundless summit, and we cannot and are not obliged to appreciate the true nature of God and His qualities. The only thing we are capable of and obliged to do is to believe in the "existence" of God and His qualities by carefully examining the world and the traces of the divine grandeur. But the true nature of God and His qualities has never been known and will never be! And we should never imagine that because as our religious leaders have observed, "Anything that we might imagine, that is not God but the gment of our imagination, and it will return to ourselves."

God is All-Hearing and All-Seeing

"Sami' and Basir" are equivalents of capable of hearing and seeing. It means that He is aware of the things that could be seen or heard, just as He is aware of the creatures and all of them are present before Him. Of course, humans see and hear by means of eyes and ears, but when it is said that God is All-hearing and All-seeing it does not mean that he has eyes and ears. But it means that God, the Exalted, is cognizant of all that could be seen or heard and everything is manifest before Him and it is evident that His awareness of all these does not necessitate eyes or ears.

Regarding this, Imam as-Sadiq ('a) has said, "When it is said that God is All-hearing and All-seeing, it does not mean that He, like us, has eyes and ears but He can see without eyes and hear without ears."[5]

Now you might ask, why should God be All-hearing and All-seeing? The answer to this question is very simple, because as we earlier noted God enjoys limitless knowledge and is aware of "everything." And this knowledge and awareness presuppose cognizance of anything that could be seen or heard.

---

[5] 'Usul al-Ka, vol.1, Akhundi, p.109.

Therefore, to establish these two qualities (All-hearing and All-seeing) we don't need two distinct set of reasons. Furthermore, as was noted earlier, the Creator should possess the great qualities and be free from any shortcoming and seeing and hearing, in the sense that was explained are great qualities whose absence would accordingly constitute an imperfection.

The unity of God could be established in manifold manners but in this lesson we will present two of them.

The First Argument

The solidarity and coordination of the universe by itself is a strong evidence of God's unity. Imagine that there is a ve-hundred-page book before you which you have not yet read. As yet you don't know whether it is the work of the mind and pen of one author or each section of the book has been written by one separate writer.

To establish this, you will have to read the entire book. If you realize that the spirit of the contents, the style of the arguments and organization of the sentences are unied and harmonious, you will denitely conclude that the whole book is written by one writer, because if it were co-authored by two or more authors, you would have come up with a difference. No matter how subtle, hidden, and insignicant that difference is, so that it won't be discovered by laymen, it won't evade the scrutiny of experts who will gure out that the book is not the work of one person.

Given this introduction, we begin studying the universe which has been called "God's book" by some scientists. We will consult the experts of every science pertinent to the world to see whether all the pages of this magnicent book of creation are unied and harmonious or not. If it so, it will be the strongest testimony to the unity of its Creator.

In fact, when we pose this question to the scientists of these disciplines, they reafrm the unied order that is prevalent throughout the world and they contend that this world is founded upon a unied plan and its rules are so encompassing, comprehensive and harmonious that an experiment with a single creature would reveal a general rule that is valid everywhere. All scientists, including biologists, physicists, and astronomers attest to the existence of this harmony and coordination.

Could harmony and similarity be more obvious than this that the solar system and other gigantic systems are subject to the same rule to which the tiny atom is subject. As we all know, the revolution of the big planets around their orbits results from two forces, viz. "gravity" and "centrifuge." Atoms, hundreds of millions of which don't take up more than a millimeter, also have these two forces of "gravity" and "centrifuge." As a result of these forces, "electrons" revolve around "protons."

If you look at the world of plants, animals and humans, you will come across the same harmony. The general rule of reproduction among plant, animals and humans is so similar to one another that it has led some to conclude that "All species, in principle, spring from one specimen." Could not you gure out that excerpts from different speeches extracted from a number of recordings have been delivered by one person? You could establish the fact that by means of investigating the coherence, cohesion, the similarity of style and structures.

The world is like a book composed of many pages, whose every page and line has been examined and studied by thousands of scientists. All unanimously concur that the entire length of the book is subject to series of general rules. For instance, the rule of causality is valid everywhere or the rule of gravity could be applied to the entire world of substance. All atoms have a center and the rule of light is the same everywhere.

Does not the harmony and coordination observed in the book of creation attest to the unity of its Creator? Do not you think it likely that if the world had two or more creators, it would result in diversity and discordance in the management and maintenance of the world?

Hisham, one of the youngest and most outstanding disciples of Imam as-Sadiq ('a) asked him, "What is the reason for the unity of God?"

The revered Imam summarized the above-mentioned argument in a concise sentence, "The continuity and coordination of the world (that are inextricably linked to one another) and the integrity and perfection of the creatures testify to the unity of the Creator."[6]

---

[6] Al-Tawhid by al-Saduq, p.250.

The Second Reason for the Unity of God

The second reason for the unity of God is the fact that all the prophets sent to guide people who proved their authenticity with miracles and innumerable signs, encouraged people to worship the Only God and practice monotheism without any exception. It goes without saying that if there were more than one god, the prophets would not invite people to practice monotheism but would direct people to the gods by whom they were appointed. And it is quite baseless to argue that there might be gods who have not sent any prophets to guide their creatures. How is it probable that God could have been so indifferent to his most superior creature (man) and neglect to send any leader or guide to lead him toward prosperity.

The Commander of the Faithful in a letter to Imam Hasan ('a) has raised the same point. "O dear son! Know that if there were any god except the Only God, it must have sent prophets. And the fact that all the prophets invite us to worship the Only God, strongly testies to the fact that there is no god except the Only God. Besides, if God had any partner, the traces of his divine dominion and rule would be evident, when no such vestige could be traced, we are reassured that God has no partner.[7]

Defective attributes are those whose presence in a person reveals his deciency and imperfection. And God is free from any quality that presupposes shortcoming and need. To clarify this, we will examine some of these.

God is Not Material

It is obvious that any material needs some space and if God were material, it would take up some space and as we learned earlier, God is needless because the needy and the dependent could not be Creator who must be capable of meeting any need. Therefore, God is not material because materials need space.

God is Not Compounded

God is not compounded because any compound needs its components. For example, a compounded medicine or an alloyed metal which is made up of certain parts needs those components and if one of the components were missing, that medicine or metal would not be.

Similarly, if the nature of God were composed of a number of components, it would be in need of its parts and as we earlier pointed out dependence and necessity are not consistent with godhood which entails absolute abundance and needlessness.

God Could Not be Seen with Eyes

The quality of being seen is contingent upon certain conditions including materiality and occupation of space. Unless these conditions

---

[7] Nahj al-Balaghah, vol. 3, Egypt, p. 49.

are met, the thing cannot be seen with eyes even with the help of equipment. Having demonstrated the fact that God is not material and neither does he occupy space, accordingly it is proven that it could not be seen with eyes.

It could not be claimed that anything that could not be seen with eyes does not exist. Just as there are certain things which are invisible but nonetheless exist (like electric waves) and their existence could be found out through their effects. Thus, every being should not be necessarily seen and it could not be said that anything which is invisible does not exist.

God Does Not Need Anything in Any Way

If God's nature were needy and dependent, there would be no distinction between Him and other creatures. That is, just as, every creature needs another thing to fulll his needs, if God were needy, this would be true of Him as well, and He would need another god to fulll His needs. Therefore, it should be said that, basically necessity and need are not compatible with "godhood", because God is the one who meets all needs and anything that is needy and dependant could not fulll others' needs. Concerning this, the Holy Qur'an says,

> "O man, you (and every creature) are in need of God and He is the only one who is absolutely needless and abundant" (The Holy Quran, Surah al-Fatir 35:15).

Earlier we read that the Creator should possess all the great qualities and should be free from all shortcomings and defects. One of the great qualities of God is *justness*. Because anyone who exercises tyranny and oppression is either ignorant of its evil nature or deems himself needy and does so to meet his needs. For instance, someone who seizes other peoples' properties by force is either ignorant of the viciousness of this act or he tries to fulll his needs or eliminate his lack of wealth that he regards as a defect.

But with regard to the Creator of the world who is absolutely needless and the source of all virtues and is acquainted with the true nature of everything through His boundless knowledge, it is quite absurd to be tyrannical and oppressive. In some prayers we read,

"O God! Anyone who exercises oppression is weak and impotent, and he does so to make up for his weakness. But Your Holy and Lofty Being is free from such defects."[8]

Note

The reason why the Shi'ahs regard justness as the second primary principles of their religion is that some Sunni sects do not consider justness necessary for God. That is, they argue that if God, the Exalted, hurl His obedient and devout servants into hell, this would not be oppression and injustice. Even if it was deemed to be unfair, when done by God, it would not be regarded as evil. They have also raised some points on *free will and predestination* that presuppose injustice in God.

As opposed to these groups, the Shi'ahs and some other Sunni sects have proved the quality of justness in God with irrefutable reasons and have contended that without doubt, oppression and injustice are derogatory and evil and if they were committed by God, they would continue to be so, and we all know that God will never commit any evil.

Therefore, *justness* occupies the second place in the primary principles of the Shi'ahs to distinguish them from these groups of Sunni sects. Imam as-Sadiq ('a) has observed,

"God, the Exalted, won't punish the innocent due to the sins commit-

---

[8] Misbah al-Mujtahid, p. 188.

ted by others and He won't torment children due to the transgressions and sins perpetrated by their parents. God, the Exalted, can forgive sins and it is beneath God to exercise tyranny and oppression."⁹

The third primary principle is the faith in the prophetic mission of the prophets who were sent by God to guide and lead mankind and as some sources suggest the number of these prophets amounts to 124,000. The last prophet after whom no other prophet has come or will ever come is Muhammad ibn 'Abdullah (may God bless him and his household) who introduced Islam.

---

9 Al-Tawhid by al-Saduq, p. 407.

The Necessity of the Appointments Of Prophets

It is evident that the All-wise Creator did not create this vast universe in vain and also it is obvious that the goal behind creation is not protability because as we noted previously God is free from any defect and need and so He did not create the world to fulll His needs and complement Himself. Consequently, the objective behind creation must have to do with the creatures. And the only objective that one could imagine for this world is the evolution and perfection of the creatures, especially the all-out evolution of mankind. Now, this question arises that how and by what means this all-out evolution could be accomplished?

It is manifest that the evolution and progress of mankind is not practicable without a divine plan and instructor. Because earthly leaders due to their limited knowledge and perceptions could not direct mankind accurately, and since they are not free from error and mistake and their judgments are erroneous, they are not qualied to assume leadership unless they follow heavenly leaders.

But the divine leaders, thanks to their connection with the Unseen and their freedom from error and mistakes can direct mankind toward genuine prosperity without lapsing into error in their leadership.

Given what was said earlier, one realizes that mankind's plan must have been developed by the Creator who is aware of all their needs and also knows that what is harmful and benecial for them. And these divine plans are delivered by those who are qualied for the prophetic mission and are in touch with the Unseen.

Man is Social

Every one believes that man is social, that is, he cannot keep on living on his own but has to live with other people. And this co-existence builds up the society. Undoubtedly, this way of life will lead to differences and enmities. If there were no accurate and fair law to manage the society, the society would not advance on the path of progress and prosperity.

Therefore, the vital signicance of a solid, accurate, and fair law to guard the rights of the society and individuals is evident. Now the question is who should draw up this law? Who is the best law-maker? And what are his qualications?

The rst qualication is that the law-maker should be aware of the mental, physical, emotional and instinctive traits of those to whom the law would be applied and such perfect awareness is not possible for anyone except God, because He is the creator and only He is truly aware of the internal as well as the external dimensions of mankind and their mental and physical peculiarities. Only God is cognizant of the various incidents happening in man's life and the developments occurring in the society and therefore, only He is able to draw up a perfect plan for man's life and keep him from annihilation.

God, the Exalted, has presented this plan through outstanding and eminent men picked from among people, who are free from error, so that man may achieve his all-out evolution by seeking guidance from this plan.

Another function performed by the prophets is that they are the rst to apply the divine law, that is, besides delivering the law, they teach men to practice the law. They are the visible embodiments of that law so that others choose the divine law as the plan for their lives by modeling them. Therefore, the faithful people believe that God has sent prophets to direct men toward the path of evolution and felicity in every era.

Someone asked Imam as-Sadiq ('a) "Why prophets are appointed?"

The revered Imam replied, "having proven with irrefutable arguments the existence of an All-wise Creator who has brought us form non-being to being and having established that God is not material and is superior to every other creature, and none can see or observe Him, so that he might talk to Him about the state of affairs, and put his questions to Him, therefore, it is inevitable that He must have messengers and prophets who guide people toward felicity and explain what is harmful for them and in every era, there must be a guide among people so that earth is not bereft of God's proof.[10]

We learned that prophets have been sent to lead and direct mankind. Undoubtedly, if the leader is tainted by wrongdoing and evil, he won't be able to direct people to chastity and purity. Therefore, prophets must be free from wrongdoing and mistakes, so that people may condently follow them to prosperity.

In other words, if someone urges people to be truthful and trustworthy but himself is a liar or at times lapses into dishonesty and treachery, his words will never deeply sway people. Similarly, if divine prophets had not been free from error and mistakes, and people had anticipated

---

[10] 'Usul al-Ka, vol. 2, p. 168.

that they would make mistakes in carrying out their mission, they would never have wholeheartedly believed his words.

Consequently, a complete compliance would not have occurred and their objectives would not have been achieved.

Indeed, God won't choose anyone who is not free from idolatry and wrongdoing to deliver His message. Rather, He would pick those who are free from any impurity whatsoever and would maintain this infallibility in the future to assume this lofty position.[11]

---

[11] This has been deduced from a narration from Imam al-Ridha cited in 'Uyun Akhbar ar-Ridha, vol. 2, Qum, p.125.

Prophets Must Perform Miracles

Anyone with a healthy nature, won't accept any claim without any reason, and if someone buys a claim without compelling reasons, this reveals his lack of common sense. Therefore, it is inevitable that prophets should present some evidence to prove the authenticity of their prophetic mission as well as the fact that they are sent by God.

One of the emblems that establish the prophets' connection with the Unseen is *miracles*. *Miracle* signies something that could not be performed by others except the prophets. For example, reviving the dead or curing incurable diseases. With regard to this, Imam al-Sadiq ('a) has said, "Any prophet should present some proof of his honesty."[12] And one of the most manifest proofs is *miracles* through which people can establish the authenticity of anyone who claims to be a prophet.

As we said the last prophet is Muhammad ibn 'Abdullah. He was appointed as prophet at the age of forty. As attested by history, throughout his life he never ever worshipped idols or abandoned his faith in God. Prior to his appointment, he occasionally went to a certain

---

[12] 'Usul al-Ka, vol. 1, p. 168. It is likely that the word 'alam be read as 'ilm.

location in Hara Mountain (Hara cave) during certain seasons to serve and worship the Only God.

He was appointed by God to lead people with the divine plans and rules at a time when the contemporary society was gripped by chaos, bloodshed, conicts, and superstitions and when myths prevailed in the minds.

He proclaimed his invitation and to prove his authenticity he presented innumerous signs and miracles. Among his miracles, one was very lively, eloquent and enduring which in terms of its testimony to his prophetic mission has preserved its validity. This living evidence and immortal miracle is the Great Qur'an which still shines like a brilliant sun and lights up the hearts of its followers. Qur'an still clearly states, *"My carrier is not an ordinary person and I am not produced by his thought, rather, the person who brought me is a distinguished individual who has been in touch with the Unseen and God has sent him to guide mankind."*

The prophet of Islam has observed, "O folks! I have been appointed by God and this Qur'an is a living testimony to my prophetic mission. If you doubt me, get together and with the help of one another present one verse like one of this Qur'an. If you succeed and could equal me, then you're entitled to decline my invitation but if you fail —which you will ever do— then realize that I am a mediator between God and mankind and am God's prophet and messenger to lead you toward perfection and felicity."

At that time, all the eloquent orators and celebrated poets who were reputed to be peerless masters of eloquence failed to introduce a verse like one of Qur'an's and they acknowledged their failure and defeat. Since then, the enemies of Islam have utilized every means available against Islam but they have failed to counteract the Holy Qur'an and present one verse like that of Qur'an's.

The Qur'an, the Immortal Miracle

Qur'an is a miracle not only by virtue of its eloquence, spiritual appeal, and beauty of composition but also due to many other aspects. Now we briey allude to some of them.

1. All historians unanimously agree that the noble Prophet of Islam was illiterate and prior to his appointment at forty, had not been educated. Given this, the Muslim Prophet has recounted the accounts of a large number of the preceding prophets. Of course, the narration of other prophets' accounts per se is not a miracle. But these narratives have been incorporated by the Jewish and Christian Scriptures (the Old and New Testaments).

Therefore, we can compare this section of Qur'an (the narratives of the previous prophets) with its counterpart in the Old and New Testaments and thus establish the heavenly nature of *the Holy Qur'an*. Because having studied the current Old and New Testaments[13], we realize that their writers have presented the history of these prophets, who were prominent men and devout instructors and their accounts must be instructive, in the form of superstitious myths and have so distorted facts that in these books prophets have been depicted as inferior to ordinary men. But when we return to Qur'an, the accounts of these virtuous prophets have been presented in a way that they bear an educational and moral point for everyone.

By the same token, one cannot claim that the prophet of Islam has borrowed the contents of the Holy Qur'an from the Scriptures of the Jews and Christians to present them in the form of the Holy Qur'an.

When the Holy Qur'an recounts the story of a prophet, it also refers to a number of moral facts and points and relates their accounts without any distortion or superuous superstitions. If the prophet's source for Qur'an were not from Revelation, then undoubtedly, in recounting these stories, he would suffer from the same superstitious distortion that befell the writers of the Scriptures of the Jews and Christians and Arab storytellers and consequently the narratives of the prophets would be marred by superstitions and untruths.

You can ascertain this by comparing the accounts of Adam, Eve, Abraham and Jesus in Qur'an and the Bible. This cursory comparison will demonstrate that the Prophet of Islam has come up with these facts through divine revelation. These stories have been so blatantly distorted in the Old and New Testaments that pen is ashamed of ascribing such stories to the divine instructors whereas the same accounts have turned up in Qur'an with the best of themes bearing a series of moral and educational facts.

---

[13] Note: the present Jewish and Christian Scriptures are not those that were introduced by the prophets Moses and Jesus (peace be upon them) and the authentic scriptures are lost.

Another way of establishing the miraculous nature of the Holy Qur'an is through the rules that are included within it. These rules are so precise, robust and calculated that the passage of time and transformation of societies have never been able to undermine them. Qur'an has presented a special economic system for the human society which is capable of meeting peoples' demands in every period. If we only comply with one of the economic principles of Islam, that is, *the ban on usury* then many of the class divisions would disappear.

An illiterate person would never be able to present partially correct economic system, let alone an accurate economic system, which won't be discredited with the advent of new economic systems but its principles are endorsed by contemporary economists and which will also direct its followers (if they observe it) to elevation and dignity.

Qur'an has distributed wealth in a way that if its commands were abided by, poverty and famine would vanish. Qur'an has introduced solid criminal laws to maintain peace and welfare. The military rules and warfare principles and tactics of Islam are so progressive that they have taken into consideration the rights and sacred things of the enemy. Finally, the Islamic law is so extensive and exhaustive that it covers the entire human life from his birth to his death and has a denite verdict for even the slightest things.

Is it likely that an illiterate person could have presented such plans and enduring rules without aid form the Unseen and without any connection with God, especially in the light of the atmosphere of the time which was prevailed by ignorance and savagery?

The superiority of Islam and the miraculous nature of the Holy Qur'an are not conned to these but there are many more signs to prove that the carrier of Qur'an is a divine teacher and leader and his plan is heavenly. Imam ar-Ridha has observed, "My grandfather, Imam as-Sadiq ('a) was asked why does not the Holy Qur'an lose its appeal and originality despite its widespread progress and over-familiarity but conversely grows more lively day by day?

Imam as-Sadiq ('a) replied, "it is so because Qur'an is not exclusively pertinent to a certain time or certain people and consequently it is new and fresh all the time."[14]

Indeed, if we adopt the Holy Qur'an as our plan for life, then our perfection and prosperity will be guaranteed. And like the early Muslims who achieved dignity and splendor swiftly due to their compliance with Qur'an, we also could restore the lost grandeur of Islam. But, sadly, Muslims have abandoned Qur'an, and therefore the Muslim world is as it is.

The fourth principle of the primary principles of the religion is *the leadership of Imams.*

Imamat signies the leadership and management of the mundane and religious affairs of the people and the succession of the Prophet of Islam, Muhammad ibn 'Abdullah (S). The necessity of the succession of Imams after the Prophet is inevitable on two grounds:

1. Social life won't survive without a leader whose remarks and edicts have profound inuence. Until the Prophet was living, he was in charge of leading and ruling Muslims. It should be borne in mind that the Prophet is both a heavenly chosen messenger and the leader and ruler of Muslims.

Therefore, after the demise of the Prophet (S), his successor must immediately assume the leadership to pursue the objectives of the Prophet, that is, to spread monotheism across the globe, and lead the people to the desired end. Otherwise, the efforts of the great Prophet (S) would be voided and Muslims would be detained on their journey to perfection.

---

[14] 'Uyun Akhbar ar-Ridha, vol. 2, Qum, p. 87.

1. The great Prophet besides being the ruler and leader of Muslims, was also a divine instructor and a heavenly messenger who explained the facts to people. After the demise of the Prophet, if there were no Imam or leader who would explicate religious facts and concepts and thus carry on with the mission of the Prophet, this would constitute a shortcoming and defect in the Islamic world.

Therefore, it is vitally signicant that the Imam who is the successor of the Prophet, immediately assume the management of the affairs and fulll the needs of people in terms of religious and faith-related questions. And the meaning of the statement that the Prophet has explained the faith of Islam completely is that he has outlined the general points completely. Thus, the explication of these general points, and the elimination of ambiguities and the instructions of the lofty facts of Qur'an certainly necessitate a great instructor whose knowledge is on a par with that of the Prophet.

Now, I draw your attention to the following debate conducted between one of the students of Imam as-Sadiq ('a) and a Sunni scientist, on the necessity of Imams and leaders after the Prophet.

Hisham, one of the youngest and most prominent students of Imam al-Sadiq ('a) says, "On a Friday, I arrived in the city of Basrah, and went to the mosque. 'Amr ibn 'Ubayd Mu'tadhidi was at the mosque and a large crowd had huddled around him asking questions.

I went up and sat among them. Everyone was asking questions. I turned toward 'Amr and said, 'O the great scholar! I am not from this city; may I ask you a question?'

'Amr said, 'ask what you like.' I said, 'Do you have eyes?'

He said, 'Don't you see I have eyes; why do you ask?' I said, 'My questions are of this type.'

He said, 'Ask though they are useless.' 'Do you have eyes?'

'Yes.'
'What do you do with your eyes?'
'I look at beautiful things, and distinguish between colors and types.'
'Do you have a tongue?'
'Yes.'
'What do you do with that?'
'With that I taste the avor of food.'
'Do you have nose and the power of smelling?' 'Yes.'
'What do you do with that?'
'With that I smell the odors and distinguish between pleasing and disgusting odors.' 'Do you have ears?'
'Yeah.'
'What do you do with them?'
'With them I hear the sounds and distinguish between them.' 'Do you have heart (intelligence) besides these?'
'Yeah.'
'What do you do with that?'
'If other parts are doubtful, heart will put an end to their hesitation. Because it is evident that sensual perceptions are occasionally erroneous and to rectify their mistakes, I consult the court of my intelligence and heart.'

Hisham says, "As 'Amr ibn 'Ubayd nished there, I conrmed all his remarks and said, 'Indeed, God, the Exalted, has created the *heart* to lead the senses and rectify their errors. O great sage! Does it make sense to contend that God who has not left eyes, ears and other parts without a guide, such benecent God could have abandoned Muslims without a guide and leader after the demise of the Prophet, so that people continue to plunge into doubts and divisions and nally into destruction and annihilation? Could it be accepted by common sense?'

Hisham says, 'When I drew such a signicant conclusion from a series of simple questions, 'Amr ibn 'Ubayd understood that I am a Shi'ah and one of Imam as-Sadiq's ('a) disciples, therefore he fell silent and could not answer me and by beating around the bush he concluded the debate.'"[15]

Hisham intended to draw this conclusion from this debate that God has denitely appointed some leaders as the successors of the Prophet who will lead Muslims one after another.

Indeed, as in the words of Avicenna, the famous Muslim philosopher, "Does it sound logical that a God who has provided man with eyebrows and eyelashes and has been so solicitous in meeting the needs of mankind, to neglect his most important need, that of guidance, and abandon mankind without a guide and leader and instructor and desert people?"

Imam and the leader of the Muslims who is to succeed the great Prophet assuming the management of the mundane and religious affairs of people must have certain distinctions.

1. He must be free from errors and mistakes to be able to lead the society toward prosperity because an impure person won't be able to clean up peoples' contamination.
2. Imam must be in touch with the Unseen and enjoy boundless divine knowledge to be able to explain the Islamic facts, concepts and edicts to Muslims, because if he were to speculate or merely possess ordinary human learning like other people, then his remarks would not be compelling and people won't appreciate the truth of the Islamic teachings.
3. Imam must be appointed by the great Prophet or his predecessor on behalf of God, because none except God and His Prophet could determine the infallibility of others and people are also unable to be certain about anyone's future.

---

[15] 'Usul al-Ka, vol. 1, p. 170.

Therefore, it is not appropriate to hand over the appointment of Imams to people because, although people might regard someone as innocent and pure, in actuality, he may be the contrary or people might conrm someone's integrity in the light of present circumstances but he may lapse into error and impurity in the future.

It is only and merely God who is aware of the present and future and within as well as the without and knows who to choose to lead the society and assume the management after the great Prophet. The great Qur'an says,

> *"God knows better to whom He should turn over the religious and mundane leadership of the people"* (The Holy Quran, Surah al-An'am 6:124).

Who Has Been Appointed as the successor of the Prophet?

At the command of God, the Prophet of Islam has introduced all of his successors and has explicitly named them, one by one, and has recurrently reminded people of 'Ali's right to succession.

An examination of history and books will reveal that the Prophet over the twenty-three years of his prophetic mission has raised the subject of the succession of Imam 'Ali on any propitious occasion. Here, we will only refer to two cases, the rst took place at the onset of the prophetic mission and the second occurred during the last year of his life.

The Prophetic Mission And The Leadership Of Imams Are Continuous

Approximately three years after the appointment of the great Prophet, this verse was revealed,

"Admonish your close relatives with the threat of divine torment (and invite them to worship God)" (The Holy Quran, Surah al-Shu'ara' 26:214).

In the exegesis of this verse, the commentators have pointed out that, on the day when the great Prophet was called on by God to invite his close relatives, he asked 'Ali who was barely fteen years old to prepare food, then he invited the progeny of 'Abd al-Muttalib who numbered about forty to announce his mission to them. On that day, Abu Lahab the Prophet's uncle disrupted the reception with irrelevant remarks.

The great Prophet held another session and after the meal was served announced his invitation and said, "I have been appointed by God and herald the best of this world and the hereafter for you and God has called on me to invite you to His dominion…"

Then, at the same reception the great Prophet observed, "Who among you is ready to stand by me, to be my brother and successor?"

'Ali rose and voiced his readiness. The great Prophet told him to sit down and repeated his invitation three times. No one answered him except 'Ali, every time he announced his invitation, then he turned to those who were present and said, "This youth, 'Ali, is my brother and successor among you, obey him and listen to his remarks."

This incident, about its authenticity there is no doubt neither in the accounts of the Sunni nor Shi'ah, clearly demonstrates that the prophetic mission and the leadership of Imams are not distinct and on the day when the divine Prophet was introduced to people, it is on the same day that his successor should be named and it should be known basically that the foundations of these two positions are the same and they are connected to one another like the links of a chain and the leadership of Imams is the continuation of the prophetic mission and the successor of the Prophet pursues the same goals as the Prophet but the distinction between them is that the Prophet is the founder of the religion but Imam is its explicator.[16]

---

[16] It has been drawn and abridged from Majma'al-Bayan, vol. 7, Islamiyah, p. 206 and al-Mizan, vol. 15, p. 263 onward and some other books.

The Hadith of Ghadir

In the last year of his life, the great Prophet who was returning from the Hajj pilgrimage stopped at a place called *Ghadir* where pilgrims parted from one another. There he mounted a high mound so that he could be seen by everyone whose number amounted to nearly one hundred thousand and at the command of God announced the succession of Imam 'Ali to that crowd. He held 'Ali's hand and raised it so that everyone could observe, and then said, "O folks! Just as I am your leader and decision-maker and have control over your life and property, 'Ali is also your leader and commander."

Thus, again it was made clear to everyone that 'Ali is the immediate successor of the great Prophet and on the same day people offered congratulations to 'Ali and even 'Umar told 'Ali, "Great, you're my and every Muslim's leader."[17]

Indeed, the Prophet of Islam announced Imam 'Ali's right to succession again and again so that everyone should know who is the ruler of Muslims after the demise of that revered gure.

---

[17] The tale of Ghadir has been cited in every Shi'ah and Sunni book and for more information look at the translation of the first volume of al-Ghadir.

Hadith al-Thaqalayn

Besides these, in the nal days of his life, the great Prophet told people, "O folks! I leave you with two priceless things, that is, *Qur'an and my household,* so long as you seek these two and follow my legacy, you won't go astray."[18]

---

[18] There is no doubt about the issuance of this hadith by the great Prophet (peace be upon him and his household) neither on the part of Shi'ahs nor Sunnis, for more information consult the translation of Hadith al-Thaqalayn by Shaykh Qawam al-Din Wishnawi published in Qum and Tehran.

The Hadith of Jabir

Jabir ibn 'Abdullah Ansari recounts that when the verse, *"Obey God and the Prophet and those who are in authority among you!"* was revealed I told the divine Prophet, *"O the Messenger of God! We know God and His Prophet and it is important that we know those who are in authority with whom this verse obliges us to comply, could you explain the meaning of the phrase?"*

The great Prophet said, "they are my successors and the Imams after me and they begin with 'Ali ibn Abi Talib and then respectively, Hasan ibn 'Ali, Husayn ibn 'Ali, 'Ali ibn Husayn, Muhammad ibn 'Ali who is known as *Baqir* in the Bible and you will spend your old age in his leadership and remember me to him when you see him. After Muhammad ibn 'Ali, the rest are as follows respectively, Ja'far ibn Muhammad, Musa ibn Ja'far, 'Ali ibn Musa, Muhammad ibn 'Ali, 'Ali ibn Muhammad, Hasan ibn 'Ali, and after him his son who is my namesake and who will dominate the whole world and who will be hidden from the sight of people and whose absence will be protracted that only those who remain steadfast and rm will persist in their belief in his leadership."[19]

Of course, the accounts pertaining to the successors of the great Prophet are innumerable and we raised these just to exemplify some. Therefore, undoubtedly, the twelve Imams of the Shi'ah have been determined by the great Prophet on behalf of God and furthermore, every Imam has explicitly introduced his successor to remove any misunderstanding and doubt on the part of people.

In addition to this, as we noted earlier, Imam must be infallible and connected with the Unseen and after the great Prophet except these twelve gures, innocence has not been veried in any one and no one has been able to present teachings and insights similar to those delivered by these twelve gures. To establish this it sufces to examine *Nahj al-Balaghah* by 'Ali and the remarks recorded from other Imams.[20]

The fth principle of the primary principles of religion is the faith in *the Resurrection*.

The Resurrection signies revival to bear the consequences. This principle, that is, the faith in the Judgment Day is one of the oldest beliefs of humanity its traces could be detected in nations with an old history.

Among the well-established religions of the world, the question of an immortal life in the hereafter constitutes one of the principal doctrines and any faith on whose agenda there is no place for the faith in the resurrection could not be called a divine faith.

The records of this faith among all nations of the world could establish its inherent quality because it is improbable that such a faith with so long a history and such a widespread purview could have ourished in

---

[19] Kifayah al-Athar, first print, p. 7.

[20] Note: You will read the abridged account of the fourteen infallible gures which is in effect complementary to the discussion of the prophetic mission and the leadership of Imams after the lesson about the Resurrection.

the hearts of people unless its were inherent. At times, everyone will feel that his life won't dissolve by death and death is not the nal destination of his evolution and he has not been created for a transitory life replete with vicissitudes and disillusionments but rather this dark night will culminate in a bright daybreak and death is not but a doorway to an eternal life.

Therefore, it should be said that the faith in the Resurrection is inherent and does not need any reasoning at all, but despite that, for the sake of clarication, here we elaborate on two arguments for the necessity of *the Resurrection.*

The Relationship Between The Divine Justice And Wisdom And The Resurrection

The world inhabited by mankind is founded upon justice and fairness. Its Creator is also just and fair and has commanded His servants to base their worldly lives upon justice and refrain from oppression and He has sent infallible prophets to guide and assist them in discriminating between good and evil.

But with respect to the divine commands and the edicts of the prophets people are divided in two categories:

1. One group is submissive and obedient and never deviates from the straight path of religion and morality and tries to abstain from corruption, indecency, and wrongdoing, or at least they are determined to purify themselves.
2. Another group is so steeped in debauchery and oppression and they behave as though no prophet had ever been sent to guide them and the straight path has not been revealed to them. In their lives, the only objectives they pursue are domination, gratication of lustful

desires, deception, duplicity, and oppression and to achieve their goals; they won't spare any brutality or ruthlessness. For instance, we read in history that a certain ruler, whose name evokes fear and terror, says, "I enjoy hurling the worshippers in the re and listening to their whining and growling, because the moaning and whining of innocent people in the ames and under torture is the most melodious music." He was a human being.

As opposed to this, we come across another person who says, "I swear by God that if they granted me the dominion of the whole world to oppress a feeble ant, I will never do that." We all have known and continue to know some who do nothing but wickedness and indecency as well as those who have dedicated their welfare to that of fellow-Muslims.

Is it consistent with God's justness that these two groups be treated equally? Does the Just God to whom every conduct of His servants is manifest and who is aware of the within and without of everyone treat these two groups equally?

The common sense dictates that these two groups are different and each should face the consequences of their actions. Those who have retained their faith in God and have done deeds of righteousness should receive their rewards and those who were non-believers and were contaminated by oppression and wrongdoing should face the consequences of their viciousness. Indeed, God's justice dictates that there must be a distinction between the faithful and the virtuous and the unfaithful and the evil. There is no doubt that this distinction does not occur completely in this world because as we could see many indels and oppressors enjoy a luxurious life and become prosperous by exploiting others.

As opposed to this we come across some virtuous people who dedicate their lives to serving and helping others and obediently perform their individual and social obligations but are aficted by vicissitudes, indigence, torture or captivity and eventually die under these circumstances.

Therefore, due to God's wisdom and justice, there must be a hereafter where the virtuous reap the reward of their good deeds and the vicious suffer the consequences of their evil deeds.

And this hereafter refers to the Resurrection which is stressed in every divine religion especially Islam, in which it is presented as one of the primary principles of the faith.

The God in whom we believe is All-wise an All-knowing and His actions arise from wisdom and He pursues some objectives in creating this world and mankind and endowing man with the faculty of thought and sending magnicent prophets to enlighten them.

Is the objective behind the creation of man limited to this life in which man might fulll his whims and gratify his hunger and thirst and nally die after a life of luxury or deprivation?

If the objective of creating mankind is conned to this, it should be confessed that his creation is futile and if the Creator of the universe is All-wise, He won't do anything aimlessly.

With a little reection and contemplation, we reach the conclusion that the aim of creating mankind is not conned to this transient life but rather he has been created for an eternal and immortal life that is the same as the hereafter. The great Qur'an has raised this argument and reads,

> *"Do you suppose that you have been created aimlessly and you won't return to Us" (The Holy Quran, Surah al-Mu'minun 23:115).*

The Resurrection is Corporeal

As it is learned from the Holy Qur'an, the resurrection and revival is corporeal, that is, the spirit is restored to the body and the soul and the body both face the consequences of their deeds.

One day, one of the opponents of Islam called *Ubay ibn Khalf* brought a rotten bone to the Prophet and crushed it into powder and scattered the powder and tried to use this to deny the Resurrection and show the impossibility of the scattered powder's restoration to its original form, and said, "What power can revive these rotten bones?"

God, the Exalted, commanded the great Prophet to say this in response, "The same God who fashioned these bones from dust in the rst place and bestowed life and vivacity upon them, He is capable of restoring these rotten bones which are scattered everywhere and reviving them."

"Ubay ibn Khalf says, 'Who will revive these rotten bones?' O our messenger! Tell him,

> *"The One who initially created them and endowed them with life will revive them."* (The Holy Quran, Surah Yasin 36:79).

The Implications of the Faith in the Resurrection

The faith in the Resurrection enhances one's diligence and determination in fullling their obligations because one knows that no action will be overlooked and God is a meticulous and fair judge who is aware of the within and without of everyone and thus he will retain his hope and resolve in serving and reforming himself.

The faith in the Resurrection heralds an eternal life and one knows that he is not created for this ephemeral life and with death he enters a new phase of life which is substantially vaster than this worldly life and he recognizes that this life is the preamble to the life in the hereafter and that eternal life will be shaped by one's conduct and deeds in this life and in other words, he will reap what he has sown in this life. Regarding this, the great Qur'an says,

> "Anyone who performs a good deed even if this weighs as much as a little seed, he will receive its reward, and anyone who commits a sin, even if that weigh as little as a seed, he will suffer the consequences" (The Holy Quran, Sura al-Zalzala, 99:7-8).

Muhammad was born on Rabi'al-Awwal 17, in the year when the story of the elephants and the destruction of the army of Abrahih[21] took place.

His father passed away prior to his birth and his grandfather 'Abd al-Muttallib adopted him. At the age of six, his mother Aminah died and two years later, he lost his grandfather, 'Abd al-Muttallib, and then his uncle Abutalib adopted him. He married Khadijah when he was twenty five years old.

He lived among people with so much honesty, trustworthiness, and magnanimity that everyone called him *the trustworthy Muhammad* and they had so much confidence in him that on great social occasions and whenever a dispute took place, they sought his judgment, during these forty years (prior to his appointment), he had no preoccupation except worshiping God and serving people. Every year, he spent some time in a cave called *Hira'* and there he worshipped God with reflection upon His signs.

The Commander of the Faithful in his book *Nahj al-Balaghah* observes, "God had commanded one of His greatest angels to wait on the great Prophet who kept him company day and night and guided him in the virtues and good deeds."

At the age of forty, he was appointed to the prophetic mission. The first man to accept his invitation was 'Ali and the first woman to do so was his wife Khadijah and for a long time only these two individuals said prayers along with the Prophet.

Saudi Arabia, at that time, was bereft of science, culture, and civilization and bloodshed, indecency, atrocity, and pillage were ubiquitous.

---

[21] Abrahah, the emperor of Yemen with a large army and a number of fighting elephants arrived in Mecca to destroy Ka'bah but thanks to a divine miracle and by means of birds which dropped stones on them, they were defeated and could not demolish Ka'bah. This story has been cited in chronicles and surah Elephant of the Qur'an alludes to this story.

The great Prophet set out to guide and lead people toward God in such a bleak environment and suffered so much in this cause that we could never imagine.

For example, we read in history that following the demise of the revered Abutalib, the great Prophet set out on a journey to Ta'if to guide the dwellers of that city. There, the respected citizens did not accept his invitation and besides that, they abused him and the thugs of the city, having realized that he was not respected by the senior members of the city, lined up on both sides of his path and pelted so many stones at his legs that they were covered with blood and were severely injured.

The great Prophet spent thirteen years in Mecca after his appointment and then immigrated to Medina where he laid the foundations of the global Islamic rule and spent the rest of his life, that is, ten years, there. He was solely preoccupied with the advancement of the community and familiarizing people with God and spirituality and eventually passed away ten years after immigration at the age of sixty three and was buried in Medina.

The Great Prophet's Conduct

The Prophet was the wisest, most knowledgeable, most patient and kindest of all people. He always sat on the ground and ate his meals there and helped in household chores, for example, he occasionally answered the door himself. He drew milk form the sheep himself and helped his servant when he got tired of spinning the manual mill (which was kept at home then).

He never lost his temper due to mundane affairs and his fury and anger were aroused only because of God. He consorted with the poor and working classes and shared meals with them and he honored the learned and the righteous.

He never exercised discrimination between himself and his servants in food and clothing. He never abused anyone. He greeted everyone he saw and he remembered God wherever he was. He mostly sat facing Ka'bah. If anyone needed his help, he swiftly went to help out. He honored guests and at times he spread his cloak on the ground so that the guest could sit on it.

One day, a person talking with the Prophet was trembling and shuddering out of his greatness and nobility, the Prophet said, "why are you afraid of me, I am not a despot (I am a God's servant like you)."

The people of Hijaz attached no importance to women and they even buried their female babies but the great Prophet offered much advice concerning women and saved them from captivity and misfortunes.

Drinking liquor, adultery, indecency, gambling and a variety of other sins were widespread among people but thanks to the sacrices of the great Prophet, they were eradicated and a population which was deprived of everything attained a power that could save the two powerful kingdoms of the time (Iranian and Roman) from the yoke of oppression and make them acquainted with Islamic teachings.

In whatever he did, he solely relied on God and his faith and he always urged people to take steps in the cause of God and for His satisfaction.

In one of the conicts, the great Prophet was separated from his companions by a long distance. He was noticed by one of the foes sitting at one corner. He picked up his sword and rushed toward him and said, "O Muhammad! Who can save you from me now?"

The great Prophet said condently, "God." As the Prophet uttered this word, that man's hands began trembling and his sword fell. Then the great Prophet took his sword and said, "Who will save you from me now?" The man said, "No one, because I don't believe in your God to seek help from Him, " and subsequently he professed his belief in God and testied to the prophetic mission of him.[22] Indeed, anyone who has faith in God, He will help him under all circumstances and will save him.

'Ali was born on Rajab 13, thirty years after the destruction of the elephants, in the House of God, Ka'bah. He was ten, when the great Prophet was appointed and during the twenty three years of his mission, he always stood by him and spared no sacrice in the cause of God and the great Prophet. His sacrices and his efforts in the cause of Islam especially at times when Islam was seriously threatened on all sides are

---

[22] Abu'l-Futuh exegesis, vol. 4, Islamiyah, p. 138.

unforgettable.

On the night, when the indels had plotted to raid the house of the Prophet and kill him, the Prophet told 'Ali, "The indels have decided to break into my house and kill me and God has commanded me to leave Mecca and ask you to sleep in my stead. Are you ready to do so?"

'Ali said, "If I sleep in your bed, will you be safe?" The great Prophet replied, "Yes."

'Ali prostrated himself to thank God and said, "May my life be sacriced to yours, I willingly comply with whatever you command and pray God for success."

In all battles, he span around the Prophet like a buttery and faced many dangers to keep him safe. In every way, he was identical to the great Prophet as if he were his reection in the mirror.

The great Prophet has said, "I am the city of knowledge and 'Ali is like the gate to this city and anyone who seeks entry to acquire knowledge must do so through 'Ali."

The great Prophet has also observed, "'Ali is with truth, and truth is with 'Ali and these two will never part from one another and whatever 'Ali says is truth and whatever way he species is the path of truth."

Although he was inalienably entitled to succeed the Prophet[23] following the demise of the Prophet his undeniable right to succession was violated, nevertheless to preserve the foundation of Islam, 'Ali never, during the twenty years when he was robbed of his right, did anything that might divide the Muslim community and thus afford Islam's foes the opportunity to destroy it but rather he did his best to help Islam and Muslims and did not withhold his guidance on important occasions. Finally people pledged allegiance to him as the ruler in the year 35, and his rule lasted ve years until in the Ramadhan of the year 40, he was martyred at the mosque of Kufah. May God bless him! His holy shrine

---

[23] This was discussed in lesson thirteen, reread that carefully.

is located in Najaf which is one of the cities of Iraq.

'Ali's Will

Excerpts from the Commander of the Faithful's recommendations to his son, Imam Hasan ('a).

Say your prayers on time and pay your alms taxes (*zakat*) punctually and under any circumstances, whether you feel pleased or angry or furious, observe the golden mean. Be friendly to the needy and consort with them.

O my son! Endeavor in the cause of God and don't quit recommending decency and forbidding indecency. Behave in a brotherly manner toward your fellow-Muslims for the sake of God. Remember God all the time. Be kind to children, and respect the elderly. Don't eat any food unless you have already given some part of it away to the needy. [24]

---

[24] Al-Amali by Shaykh Tusi, first print, p. 4.

The Woman Who Introduced 'Ali to Mu'awiyah

After the martyrdom of the Commander of the Faithful ('a) Sudah, the daughter of 'Ammarah called on Mu'awiyah (May God's curse be upon him) to complain about their governor who was appointed by him. Mu'awiyah did not heed her protest and threatened to send her to the same ruler to be at his mercy.

Sudah bowed her head for a while and then raised it and recited this verse,

"May God bestow His blessing upon the body which when it was placed in the grave, justice was buried simultaneously, too."

"The one who was allied with truth and was inextricably linked to faith and truth." Mu'awiyah said, "Perhaps you mean 'Ali."

She said, "Yes, I mean 'Ali ('a)". Then she recounted her memory of that Imam, "During his rule, we were oppressed by one of his appointees, we expressed our discontent to 'Ali. Having listened to our complaint, he started crying and said, "O God you bear witness that I have never told them to wrong people." And he immediately sacked that oppressive appointee.[25]

Fatimah ('a) was born on Jumada al-Thani 5, ve years after the appointment of the Prophet from Khadijah. At the age of ve, her mother passed away. The great Prophet loved his daughter so much that he used to say "Fatimah is the dearest and most respected of people to me."

Fatimah's stature in terms of great human attributes, and virtues, and God's worship was so high that whenever she went to the Prophet's house, she was welcomed and greeted by him and he kissed her hand and gave his place to her and about her he has said, "Fatimah is my esh, whoever pleases her has pleased me and whoever offends her has offended me."

Imam Hasan ('a) recounts that, "On a Friday night, my mother, Fatimah, was engaged in worshipping God and saying prayers nonstop until daybreak but she prayed for other people most of the time. I told her, 'O mother! Why don't you pray for yourself?' She replied, 'O my son! First neighbors, then ourselves.'"[26]

One day, the great Prophet asked, "What is the best thing for women?"

Fatimah ('a) replied, "O Father! It is best for women not to be seen by strange men and not to see a strange man." The great Prophet embraced her and said, "Offspring and generation that some spring from some."[27] That is, Fatimah is the daughter of the Prophet and has obtained her excellence from him.

Indeed, today when the societies are suffering from the consequences of mixing the sexes and their unrestricted relationship, they appreciate the true meaning of Fatimah's remarks that the only way through which the society might be kept from corruption and depravity is to segregate the sexes at work and at school, otherwise, the society will plunge deeper

---

[25] Al-Fosul al-Muhimmah, Tehran, p. 129 and Sanah al-Bihar, vol. 1, p. 672.

[26] Kashf al-Ghummah, vol. 2, 25.

[27] Bayt al-Ahzan, 12 and Kashf al- Ghummah, vol.2, 23 with slight difference.

and deeper into corruption and decadence.

Fatimah ('a) died at the age of eighteen. For nine years she lived with 'Ali and bore children like Imam Hasan, Imam Husayn, and Zaynab for the Muslim community. Eventually, approximately three years after the demise of the great Prophet, she passed away in Medina and was secretly buried overnight.[28] During these three months, she did her best to defend 'Ali's right to succession and leadership and nally sacriced her life for the same cause.

It was on Ramadhan 15, 03 that Imam Hasan ('a) was born from such a great mother as, Fatimah ('a). He was the rst child who beamed in the house of leadership. As the great Prophet was informed of his birth, he went to the house of 'Ali and Fatimah and took his daughter's baby and embraced him and then recited *Adhan* in his right ear and *Iqamah* in his left ear and subsequently, at the command of God, called him Hasan.

One of his most famous epithets is *Mujtaba*. Imam Hasan was raised by such exemplary parents as 'Ali and Fatimah and the marks of greatness and magnanimity were evident in him from early on. The great Prophet liked him so much and regarding him has observed, "O God! You know that I like Hasan and also like anyone that likes him."

He has also observed, "Hasan is my blossom" and also that, "Hasan and Husayn are the leaders of Muslims whether they rise up or not." That is, even if for the sake of Islam they decide to remain silent and refuse to protest against others' rule.

As children, once he and his brother Husayn saw an old man performing the ablutions incorrectly. They wanted to correct the old man but since he was aged, they did not want to do so offensively.

They staged an interesting scene. They went up to him and told

---

[28] It was done so at her request, and she did so to remind Muslims of her dissatisfaction with the events that took place after the death of the Prophet. She voiced her protest through these ways to be recorded and enlighten the Muslims.

him, "O old man! We both perform ablutions, you observe and judge who does so better!" The old man looked as they performed ablutions and realized that his own ablutions have been wrong and these great children have done that to teach him. Then he told them, "O the darlings of the Prophet! You perform ablutions correctly but my ablutions were not correct and I learned from you how to do it accurately."[29]

Imam Hasan was seven when the Prophet passed away and then he spent thirty years with the Commander of the Faithful and attained the position of leadership at the age of thirty seven. He was poisoned to martyrdom at the age of forty seven and was buried at Baqi' cemetery in Medina.

---

[29] 1. Bihar al-Anwar, vol. 43, p. 319.

Some Remarks by Imam al-Hasan

Anyone who frequents a mosque will derive one of the following benets (the mosques should have such features).

1. He will learn the primary principles of the faith and other Islamic teachings.
2. He will hear remarks that will lead him to the straight path and keep him from deviation.
3. Out of the dread of God or shyness or embarrassment, he will avoid wrongdoing.
4. He will come across a helpful brother (a faithful and close friend).
5. He will be blessed by God.[30]

---

[30] Tohaf al-'Uqul, p. 235. this narration has been quoted from the Commander of the Faithful and Imam al-Husayn (peace be upon them) in Wasa'il al-Shi'ah.

Imam Hasan's Peace Agreement

Following the martyrdom of the Commander of the Faithful, the shi'ah people of Iraq and the four thousand troops of 'Ali ('a) who had gathered at *Nukhaylah,* pledged allegiance to Imam Hasan ('a). Having concluded the allegiance ceremony, Imam Hasan delivered a critical and moving speech before a large crowd at the mosque of Kufah. During this speech, he warned people against depravity, and obedience to Satan and his followers.

Then he expressed his readiness to ght Mu'awiyah and called on the commanders of his army to get their soldiers ready for the attack on Sham and he was involved in making preparations in Kufah himself.

Mu'awiyah learned about these events and realized that Imam Hasan has decided to carry on with his father's plans. Therefore, he started sabotage and since he was adept at deception, hypocrisy, and intrigue, he managed to draw a number of Imam Hasan's companions to himself through different means and thus he drove a wedge in Imam's army. As a result of duplicity, bribery, and riches, he went so far as some of the opponents of Imam Hasan and the hypocrites and mercenaries, who were abounding in his army, wrote a letter to Mu'awiyah and promised to deliver Imam a captive, if Mu'awiyah came to Iraq.

Despite this, Imam Hasan never retracted his statements and in one of his speeches said, "Mu'awiyah along with a group of people from Sham are coming toward Kufah, you must get ready to confront them." After that he executed a spy that was sent by Mu'awiyah to Kufah and wrote to ibn 'Abbas, the governor of Basrah, to execute Mu'awiyah's spy in that city too.

Initially, people did not respond positively and at last through the encouragement and perseverance of one of his companions, they promised to assist but when Imam Hasan went to Nukhaylah, he learned that the majority of those who had pledged to help, had shrunk form their commitment and had deserted him.

Furthermore, some of his commanders joined the army of Mu'awiyah after receiving large sums of bribes at the border with Sham and abandoned Imam Hasan. In short, Imam's army was dispersed and his companions were anxious and agitated. In the meantime, a number of his enemies exploited the opportunity to attack Imam himself and plundered his tent and severely wounded his leg. This was a summary of Imam Hasan's conditions then. At this time, Mu'awiyah raised the peace agreement.

Imam Hasan ('a) thought that if he did not make peace with Mu'awiyah, both he and his companions would be slain and then Mu'awiyah would declare that they did not accept his proposal for peace and had themselves killed. Thus, he would be slain and it would not bring about any advantage for Islam and Muslims. Appreciation of the duty is more important than its fulllment. Occasionally, we are compelled to keep quiet for a long time as sages have observed, "Sometimes withdrawal is the most effective assault."

In other words, at times peace is the most honorable combat. If Imam Hasan had been swayed by the emotions of his companions, he and his companions would have been slain in vain, and he would not have derived any result from his martyrdom. Therefore, under those circumstances, Imam concluded that it is in the best interests of Islam and Muslims to accept peace, but within the framework of this peace, all the interests of Muslims should be guarded and Mu'awiyah's true nature must be exposed.

In fact, one of the wrong inclinations of some people is that, they tend to engage in warfare all the time, while on the other hand, the tendency to be constantly at peace with the enemies is also wrong. A realistic person should take into account the interests and take steps accordingly.

Sometimes, expediency compels us to wage a war and at times it dictates peace. In Islamic laws, there are rules pertinent to warfare and there are ones about peace. If the Prophet fought with the indels in the conicts of Badr and Ahzab, the same Prophet established peace with the same folks and signed the well-known Hudaybiyyah peace treaty.

Thus, at the command of God, the Exalted, Imam Hasan ('a) made peace with Mu'awiyah in a peace agreement that contained some articles. Upon closer examination of this treaty, it grows clear how far Imam took the interests of the Islamic community into account.

And the fact that Mu'awiyah did not abide by the peace agreement revealed his true nature and people more or less realized that he is not an Islamic leader but an ambitious, despotic, and secular tyrant.

The Text of the Peace Agreement

1. Mu'awiyah must conduct himself in accordance with the divine book and the tradition of the great Prophet.
2. He must refrain from reviling and maligning 'Ali ('a) and command his subordinates to abstain from abusing that Imam in their speeches.
3. He must not introduce anyone as his successor or deputy.
4. Imam Hasan ('a) should be absolved of having to call Mu'awiyah, the Commander of the Faithful.
5. He should put an end to the persecution of 'Ali's household and companions and let them live peacefully like other people.
6. He must allocate part of the revenues to Imam Hasan so that he could distribute that among the families who had lost their breadwinners in the conicts of Jamal and Sifn and also to be able to repay the debts that he had to incur for the sake of people.[31]

---

[31] Abridged from Hayat al-Hasan.

He was born on Sha'ban 3, 04. At the command of God, the great Prophet named him Husayn and foretold his martyrdom in the cause of religion on the day of his birth and said, "A group of indels and tyrants from Bani Umayyah would kill him. May God keep my intercession from them."

Husayn ('a) spent forty six years with his grandfather, parents, and brother and attained the position of leadership at the age of forty seven after the demise of Imam Hasan. He suffered under the deceptive and oppressive rule of Mu'awiyah but so long as Mu'awiyah was living, he could not do anything because just as Imam Hasan, for the sake of Islam, agreed to peace with Mu'awiyah on a number of conditions and thought it advantageous to Islam and Muslims to renounce war with him, Imam Husayn ('a) also thought it expedient to refrain from confrontation during the remaining ten years of his rule.

But following the death of Mu'awiyah, Yazid mounted the throne and announced his rule and to strengthen his position, demanded allegiance from all senior gures including Imam Husayn ('a) but Imam ('a) from the very beginning said, "When persons like the dissolute, gambling and drunken Yazid, who do not even supercially observe and respect Islam, intend to assume the leadership of the Islamic community, that time would mark the death and annihilation of Islam because these people intend to eradicate Islam with its own power."[32] And on these grounds, he refused to pledge allegiance and did not recognize the rule of Yazid and at the command of God, the Exalted, and for the sake of Islam, he decided not to acknowledge Yazid's rule and rise up against him even at the risk of his life.

Thus, upon the invitation of the inhabitants of Kufah, he set out toward Iraq in the year 60. From the start of this journey through his martyrdom, he announced to his companions and other Muslims that

---

[32] Lahuf, p. 20.

his uprising was aimed at the promotion of decency and prohibition of indecency and revolt against the oppressor and refusal to acknowledge a tyrannical regime, and eventually the protection of the Holy Qur'an, Islam and the prophetic tradition. With the same steadfast resolve, nally, he and his children and some of the youths of Bani Hashim and some of the most prominent gures of the time, were killed in Karbala and his household went into custody but he made it clear to his contemporaries and the following generations that sacrice and selessness are essential in the great cause of truth and he established his reputation like a shining sun in the history of Islam.

A Lesson From The School of Imam Husayn

Since his martyrdom, his followers and devotees have constantly commemorated his memory and have held mourning services and thus and by visiting his holy shrine they have renewed allegiance to the memory of Karbala.

Our infallible leaders underlined the preservation of the memory of Karbala and repeatedly held commemoration and mourning ceremonies themselves and talked a lot about the benets of mourning for Imam Husayn.

Abu 'Ammareh has said, "One day I was with Imam as-Sadiq ('a). He asked me to recite some elegies about Imam Husayn and as I started reading, Imam burst out crying and he kept on weeping so loudly that his cries were audible outside the house, when I nished, he talked about the advantages and greatness of reciting elegies and mourning for Imam Husayn ('a)."[33]

Indeed, mourning and crying for Imam Husayn and recalling the history of Karbala is a great virtue and is invaluable but we should

---

[33] Bihar al-Anwar, vol. 44, p. 282.

bear in mind that the mourning services and the narration of the incidents of Karbala are intended to derive lessons of seless sacrice and devoutness in the cause of religion, and the dignity and honor and protection of the Holy Qur'an and its holy edicts and not lamentation and mourning for their own sake, because the objective behind these mourning ceremonies and rites is to immortalize the goals of Imam Husayn ('a).

Excerpts From Imam Husayn's Supplications

"O God! I grant Your unity and count Your blessings although I know that I won't be able to enumerate them because Your gifts are countless."

"I have consistently, from my birthday, enjoyed Your blessings and from the start of my life, You have protected me from poverty and destitution and suffering and misery and have provided the means of my welfare."

"O the best person to whom we can express our demands, and the kindest from whom to seek forgiveness."

"O the one who is aware of the closing eyes and the secret peeping, O the one to whom the hidden secrets of the hearts are not unknown. O the kindest, bestow your good regards upon Muhammad and his household. O God! I can't accomplish but what merits my meanness and we demand what merits Your generosity."

These were the prayers that Imam said at the plains of 'Arafah on the day of 'Arafah and wept and taught greatness and knowledge of God to mankind.[34]

His name is 'Ali, the son of Imam Husayn and his most well-known epithets are Sajjad and Zayn al-'Abidin. He was born on Jumadi al-Awwal 5 or 15, 36 or 38 and attained the position of leadership after the martyrdom of his father, Imam Husayn in the year 61.

His leadership coincided with the zenith of the Umawi rule and the enemies of the prophetic household ('a) and during this period, momentous events and bloody revolts took place which entailed difculties for Imam. Occasionally, his life and at times his dignity and honor were jeopardized but with foresight, patience, fortitude, self-sacrice and self-esteem he managed to overcome all the obstacles and preserved his life and honor along with those of many others.

He was not only devout and devoted but also a thoughtful and adept leader who did his best to guard the interests of Islam and Muslims at critical moments.

One of his most outstanding services to the Islamic world and Islamic teachings is the collection of the prayers of that Imam which is known as *The Complete Sahifah-ye Sajjadiyyah*. This book and its prayers incorporate a series of rational, moral, philosophical and social facts and teachings and have been preserved in the form of supplications toward the absolutely needless. And it is impossible that anyone save an infallible Imam who has inherited the knowledge of the prophets could provide humanity with such facts and truths.

He was poisoned to martyrdom by the agents of the Umawi regime on Muharram 25, 97 at the age of fty seven or fty nine and was buried in Medina.

---

[34] Iqbal by ibn Tawus, p. 339.

Some Remarks by Imam al-Sajjad

"The dearest of you, before God, is the most righteous and the most respected of you, before God, is the most pious and god-fearing."

"O men! You will eventually die and will be revived to stand trial before divine justice, so have an answer ready."[35] That is, until the opportunity is available and you're alive get ready for the hereafter and endeavor to earn the divine pleasure.

"If all men were perished and I were deserted, I would not be terried so long as I am with the Holy Qur'an." (I will approach the Holy Qur'an and derive benets from it).[36]

He was called Muhammad and was distinguished with the epithet *Baqir al-'Ulum*, literally, explorer of sciences. His father was Imam Husayn and his mother was Fatimah, the daughter of Imam Hasan, therefore, he was directly related to Imam 'Ali ibn Abitalib through both of his parents.

He was born on Rajab 1, 47 in Medina and attained the position of

---

[35] Tohaf al-'Uqul, p. 280.

[36] Wasa'il al-Shi'ah, vol.3, p. 582.

leadership at thirty nine in 95. Since toward the end of his life, the Bani Umayyah regime had declined and was on the verge of disintegration, he managed to utilize the opportunity to explain Islamic laws and teachings to people and train innumerable students and scholars. The contemporary scholars and jurists honored him and drew benets from him.

'Abdullah ibn 'Ata has said, "I never saw scholars and scientists honor and venerate anyone as much as they did Imam Muhammad. For example, whenever Hakam ibn Utaybah, who was one of most prominent scholars of the time, met Imam, he behaved so respectfully, as if an elementary pupil behaves toward his teacher."[37]

Imam as-Sadiq ('a) has said, "My father, Imam Baqir, was always praying to God and on occasions when I walked with him, I noticed that he prayed as he walked. He was constantly worshipping God, during meals, at services with people, and he used to urge us to recite Qur'an."

Imam as-Sadiq ('a) has also observed, "Whenever my father, Imam Baqir instructed his servants to do something, he went to supervise them and if he saw they had difculty performing that, he tried to help them."[38]

Imam Baqir ('a) passed away at fty seven on Dhu'l-Hijjah 7, 114 and was buried at Baqi' cemetery in Medina.

---

[37] Al-Anwar al-Bahiyah, p. 62.

[38] Al-Anwar al-Bahiyah, p. 66.

Some Remarks by Imam Baqir

Imam Baqir told Jabir Ja'fari, who was one of his companions, "O Jabir! I swear by God that our follower (Shi'ah) is one who submits to the command of God and is pious and god-fearing. God is not biased toward anyone and the dearest servants before God are those who are the most righteous and comply with divine edicts better and more often than others. By God, the only way to please God and get closer to Him, is through obedience and submission. We cannot save you from the ames of hell. Anyone who obeys God is our companion and friend and anyone who commits sins and wrongdoings and disobeys God is our enemy. O Jabir! One cannot attain our affection but through piety and good deeds."[39]

He was called Ja'far and was known with the epithet, Sadiq. His father was Imam Baqir and his mother was Umm Farwih, who was one of the most devout women of her time. He was born on Rabi 'al-Awwal 17, 83 in Medina. He assumed leadership at the age of thirty two. He dedicated his life to educating and training thousands of students and seized the opportunity (that is, when Bani Umayyah regime was declining and

---

[39] 'Usul al-Ka, vol.2, p. 74.

ghting with Bani 'Abbas) and opened up the gates of Islamic sciences and teachings to the Muslim community.

Around 4000 people have recounted narrations from that Imam and some of them have achieved high ranks of faith and conduct.

One of them is Jabir ibn Hayyan, who is unanimously acknowledged to be the founder of chemistry. Muhammad ibn Muslim is another gure who has heard and reported thousands of *hadiths* from that Imam and the third is Hisham ibn Hakam who was the most prominent gure in rhetoric and beliefs of that time.

Mu'ali ibn khunays, who was one of the companions of the Imam, says, "On a rainy night, I noticed Imam as-Sadiq leave his house and set out toward the shelter of Bani Sa'idah where the homeless and the needy slept overnight. I also followed the Imam and all of a sudden something dropped from his hand, I went up to him and said hello. He told me to pick them up. When I bent, I realized that they were pieces of bread and I gathered them and gave them to him. He put them in a bag. I asked him to let me carry the bag but he declined and said that he was more worthy of doing that. When we arrived at that shelter, I saw a number of the poor sleeping there. He put some bread near each one of them and went past. I asked him whether they were his followers. He said if they had been his followers, he would have attended to them much more."[40]

Indeed, the great Prophet, 'Ali ('a), and other leaders constantly helped the needy and the wretched and sympathized with their misery.

Imam as-Sadiq was poisoned to death by Mansur, an 'Abbasi ruler, on the 25 of Shawwal in 148 at the age of 65. He was buried at Baqi' cemetery next to the tombs of his father, Imam Baqir, and his grandfather, Imam Sajjad, and his uncle, Imam Hasan.

---

[40] Thawab al-A'mal by al-Saduq, Ghifari, p. 173.

His Advice On Deathbed

Umm Hamidah, the magnanimous wife of Imam as-Sadiq says, "Before his death, Imam as-Sadiq opened his eyes and asked all his relatives to meet at his bed. All members of Bani Hashim got together, and then Imam glanced at them and said, "'Our intercession won't benet anyone who scorns the obligatory prayers and does not attach importance to them.'"[41]

He was called Musa and was well-known as Kazim. His father was Imam as-Sadiq and his mother was Hamidah who was very knowledgeable and Imam as-Sadiq used to ask women to consult her regarding religious edicts and teachings. He was born on Safar 7, 128, and attained the position of leadership at 21.

He spent some time in prison because Harun, the 'Abbasi ruler, deemed his presence among people dangerous and was jealous of his popularity among them and put him into jail on different pretexts. At prison, he spent his time saying prayers and worshipping God. At one of the prisons, the 'Abbasi ruler sent an attractive woman as a servant to Imam and his aim was to get Imam infatuated with that woman and

---

[41] Wasa'il ash-Shi'ah, vol.3, p. 17.

thus exploit this against him outside.

After a few days, the 'Abbasi ruler sent someone to inspect the prison and see about the Imam and the woman. He walked into the prison and saw that at one corner, Imam was engaged in prayers and at the other corner was sitting the woman praying.

The woman was taken to the ruler and was asked how come she had changed so dramatically. She replied, "Imam Kazim's routine and his devotion and devoutness inuenced and changed me." (But I could not exert any inuence upon him whatsoever).[42]

Indeed, men of God and their conduct and lifestyle attracted people toward them and they reformed and rectied the environment, and they were never swayed and corrupted by other people and the environment.

He was poisoned to death by the 'Abbasi ruler's agents and passed away in the corner of the prison of Baqdad on the 25th of Rajab of 183 and was buried at Quraysh cemetery which was later known as Kazimayn. Currently, his shrine is visited by all Muslims especially shi'ahs.

---

[42] Manaqib by Ibn Shahr Ashub, vol. 3, Najaf, p. 415.

Some Remarks by the Imam (Part One)

Anyone whose yesterday and today are equal, that is, after twenty four hours, he has not gained anything in spirituality and humanity and has not advanced on the path of piety and faith, this person is like someone who has invested but has not obtained any value in return.

And anyone who is worse than yesterday, that is, instead of spiritual progress, has deteriorated and is inclined toward wrongdoing and impiety; such a person will be far from God's grace.

The eighth infallible Imam, Ridha ('a) was born on Dhu'l-Qa'dah 11, 148 in Medina. His father was Imam Kazim and his mother was Najmah, who was one of the most prominent women of that era. He assumed leadership in 183 at the age of 36.

Concurrent with the rule of the 'Abbasi ruler, Ma'mun, and at his insistence, the Imam immigrated to Khurasan and agreed to function as his deputy. In Khurasan, he conducted debates with the scholars of other religions and all of them conceded his greatness and bowed to his knowledge and learning.

A person from Balkh says, "Once I was with Imam Ridha. He ordered to unroll the cloth for food. All the servants, even the black slaves sat at the same cloth and shared the meal with Imam. I told Imam, "It would have been better, if you did not share the meal with them." He said, "Hold it! (what is the difference between us and them) we share one God and descend from the same parents and everyone's recompense will be in proportion to his good deeds."[43]

Whenever he sat to eat food, he had already given away part of all the dishes to the poor and then started eating. At night, he slept very little and stayed up from evening to dawn.

He fasted very often and never neglected the three days of fasting every month, that is, the rst and the last Thursday of the month and the Wednesday of the middle. He went to the households of the needy, in the darkness of nights and attended to them.[44]

He was poisoned to death by Ma'mun, who was afraid of peoples' attention to him, on the last day of Safar of 203 and was buried in the city of Mashhad. Currently, his shrine is the hub of the Shi'ahs of the world.

---

[43] Al-Anwar al-Bahiyah, p. 106.

[44] 'Uyun Akhbar ar-Ridha, vol.2, p. 184.

Some Remarks by the Imam (Part Two)

God's devotion is not merely marked by the frequency of prayers and fasting but true devotion consists in man's contemplation and reection upon the religious rules to realize his duties under any circumstances and to be industrious in their fulllment.[45]

Cleanliness and sanitation are the manners of the divine prophets.[46]

Dependence on God means that man is not afraid of anything but God, the Exalted.[47]

Helping the disabled and the feeble is better than charity in the cause of God.[48]

He was called Muhammad and his best known epithets are Jawad and Taqi. His father was Imam Ridha and his mother was called Sabikah. He was born on Rajab 10, 195. He assumed leadership in 203 at the age of 9. Of course, as we noted earlier, the leadership of Imam is a divine position that is assigned by God and the Prophet and has nothing to

---

[45] Tuhaf al-'Uqul, p. 442.

[46] Ibid, p. 442.

[47] Ibid, p. 445.

[48] Ibid, p. 446.

do with age. That is, the great Prophet has determined that after the eighth leader, Imam Ridha, his son, Muhammad ibn 'Ali should succeed and therefore, Imam Ridha introduced him as the successor.

One day, when Imam Jawad ('a) entered the great Prophet's mosque, 'Ali ibn Ja'far, the son of Imam Ja'far, who was the uncle of his father was sitting there, and as Imam walked into the mosque, he rushed toward Imam barefoot and without his cloak, and bowed to him and kissed his hand and stood by him respectfully. Imam Jawad asked him to be seated. 'Ali ibn Ja'far replied, "How could I sit while you are standing?"

Following the departure of Imam Jawad ('a), some people who had witnessed this went up to 'Ali ibn Ja'far and reproached him and said, "You are the uncle of his father and he is the grandson of your brother, why do you honor him? (He should respect you) 'Ali ibn Ja'far held his white beard in his hand and said, "When God has not deemed me with my white beard worthy of the position of leadership and has regarded him deserving of the leadership despite his young age, then how do you tell me not to accept it. I seek refuge in God from what you are saying." (He is our Imam and it is incumbent upon us to submit to him and to honor him).[49]

Yahya ibn Aksam says, "One day, I entered the mosque of the Prophet and was paying tribute to his tombstone when I noticed Imam Jawad there." I posed some questions and he answered them all very well and then I said, "I have a question but I don't dare to raise it." He said, "Before posing your question, I will say it. Your questions is, who will be the leader of Muslims after my father, Imam Ridha?" I said, "By God! That was my question." He said, "After my father, I will be the Imam and God's proof."[50]

He was poisoned to death at the order of Mu'tasim 'Abbasi, on the

---

[49] 'Usul al-Ka, vol. 1, p. 322.

[50] Ithbat al-Hadat, vol. 6, p. 167 and Al-Anwar al-Bahiyah, p. 129.

last day of Dhu'l-Qa'dah of 220 at the age of 25. He was buried next to his grandfather, Imam Musa in Baqdad (Kazimayn).

Some Remarks by the Imam (Part Three)

Someone asked Imam to advise him, Imam said, "Will you take it?" He replied, "Yes." Then Imam expressed remarks with this theme,

Quit lustful desires and oppose your evil ego. Beware that God sees you constantly so watch what you are doing and how you are doing.[51]

He was called 'Ali and his best known epithets are Naqi and Hadi. Imam Jawad was his father and his mother was called Sa'idah who is said to have been peerless in piety and devoutness. He was born on Dhul-Hijjah 15, 212 and assumed leadership after his magnanimous father.

Isma'il ibn Mihran says, "When Imam Muhammad Taqi was traveling from Medina to Baghdad, I told him, 'may my life be sacriced to you! I am afraid that your life may be threatened during this trip. Who would be our leader after you?' He glanced at me and said, smiling, 'I won't die this year.' (He went to Baghdad and as he had said he returned safe). But when the 'Abbasi ruler summoned him to Baghdad again, I called on him once more and said, 'May my soul be sacriced to you! You are

---

[51] Tuhaf al-'Uqul, p. 455.

leaving, who will be the leader after you?' He cried profusely and then turned to me and said, 'I will be killed during this trip and my son, 'Ali, will succeed me as the following leader.'"[52]

Qotb Rawandi says, "Imam Hadi like his forebears possessed all the great virtues and he spent nights in praying." Among people, he always smiled and his lips were moving, praying to God.

He spent the bulk of his leadership in the city of Samarra under the surveillance of the 'Abbasi regime and nally he was poisoned to death by them on Rajab 3, 254 and at 42 and was buried in Samarra.

A man called on Imam Hadi and while trembling, timidly said, "My son has been arrested due to your friendship and they are going to kill him tonight. Imam said, "what do you want now?" The man replied, "I want what every parent desires, that is, the release of my son." Imam said, "Go, your son will be released tomorrow and will return to you." Tomorrow, his son came back and told him how he was saved from imminent death through the prayers of Imam Hadi.[53]

---

[52] 'Usul al-Ka, vol. 2, p. 323.

[53] Al-Manaqib by Ibn Shahr Ashub, vol. 3, p. 518.

Some Remarks by the Imam (Part Four)

In this world, people are evaluated by their wealth but in the hereafter, they will be assessed by their good deeds.

This world is like a bizarre where merchants and businessmen are engaged in trade, some will gain (they earn God's pleasure) and some will do poorly (with their own hands, they kindle the ames of hell for themselves).[54]

He was born on Rabi' ath-Thani 6, 232 in Medina. His father was Imam 'Ali Naqi and his mother was Salil who was the epitome of piety and devoutness. He attained leadership at 22. And like his forbears, he was poisoned to death by tyrants in 250 at the age of 28. He was buried in Samarra next to his dignied father's tomb.

He was four years old when he came from Medina to Iraq along with his father. He settled in Samarra, which is one of the cities of Iraq and he was scrutinized by the regime and was occasionally imprisoned and most of the time, he was banned from meeting people.

Isa ibn Sabih says, "When I was serving at prison, Imam Hasan 'Asqari was also brought to the prison. I took advantage of his company and at

---

[54] Tuhaf al-'Uqul, p. 483.

times, he made miraculous predictions from unknown. For example, one day he told me, 'You're sixty five years and odd month and odd days old. When I consulted my date of birth, I realized that he had told my birthday and my age exactly.'"[55]

Abu Hashim Ja'fari says, "When I was aflicted by destitution and indigence, I wanted to seek help from Imam Hasan 'Asqari but I was ashamed. When I went home, I learned that Imam Hasan 'Asqari had sent someone to my house with some money and had written a letter saying, 'whenever you are in need, ask us and do not be ashamed.'"[56]

Muntasar Billah, an 'Abbasi ruler, went to Samarra and paid tribute to the tombs of Imam 'Ali Naqi and Imam Hasan 'Asqari ('a) and left there for the tombs of the 'Abbasi rulers. They were located in a lthy, ruined and squalid neighborhood.

One of his companions told him, "You are the ruler of this country and you enjoy power and means, then why should the graves of your forbears be in such a state, that no one ever visits them and they don't have any attendants and caretakers to keep them clean and maintain them while you see that the tombs of the progeny of 'Ali ('a) (the tombs of 'Ali Naqi and Imam 'Asqari) are so tidy and clean and are decorated with carpets and curtains and lights.

Muntasar, with genuine frankness, expressed a fact and said, "This is a heavenly occurrence and is done by God, and even if we force people to honor and venerate the tombs of our family, this could not be practical, that is, people love them (the progeny of 'Ali ('a)) from the bottom of their hearts and revere them both when they are living and after their deaths but they don't like us, and while we are living respect us out of fear but as soon as we die, they won't pay attention to us, and in sum,

---

[55] Bihar al-Anwar, vol. 50, p. 275.

[56] Kashf al-Ghummah, vol. 3, p. 287.

we cannot arouse affection and devotion and conviction by force."[57]

---

[57] Kashf al- Ghummah, vol. 3, p. 437.

Some Remarks by the Imam (Part Five)

The most pious are those who avoid dubious acts (which might be forbidden) and the most devoted (faithful) are those who fully fulll their obligations and duties and the most devout are those who abstain from the forbidden and wrongdoing.

Exercise piety and conduct yourself in a way that when people realize that you are one of our followers, you may bring credit to us, and not obloquy and ignominy upon us.[58]

The arrival of a universal savior, who will transform the face of the earth and replace a world of oppression and tyranny with one of justice and fairness, has been raised in all the divine religions and their scriptures. The great Prophet, according to both Shi'ah and Sunni narrations, has said, "When the world is overowing with tyranny and oppression (and the human society is teeming with savage predators) my eleventh son who bears my name, Muhammad, and my nickname, Abu'l-Qasim, will emerge and put an end to all the iniquities and spread true Islam across the world."

The characteristics of the twelfth Imam, Hadhrat Mahdi, have been

---

[58] Tuhaf al-'Uqul, p. 488.

described in both Shi'ah and Sunni narrations; here we cite some of them:

He descends from the Prophet, 'Ali, Fatimah and Husayn. He is the ninth descendant of Imam al-Husayn, the sixth descendant of Imam al-Sadiq, the fourth descendant of Imam al-Ridha and the immediate son of Imam al-Hasan 'Askari.

He has two periods of absence, the rst one is short but the other will be very protracted. His second absence will be so prolonged that those who are not steadfastly faithful, will gradually lose faith. His lifetime will be very long.

When he emerges, he will ll the world with justness and fairness and will establish a divine rule throughout the world.

These qualications and many more have been recorded in hundreds of Shi'ah and Sunni narrations lest people be taken in by those who might introduce themselves as Mahdi by trickery and deception and be diverted from the straight path.

The twelfth Imam, Mahdi ('a) was born in 255 or 256 in Samarra. Until his father's demise in 260, many people saw him as a child at Imam al-Hasan 'Askari's household and noticed the marks of greatness and leadership in him. Imam al-Hasan 'Askari ('a) also reminded people of his prospective leadership on any propitious occasion.

Since 260, when his father passed away, he was concealed from the sight of people (because the 'Abbasi rulers intended to kill him and were rmly determined to detain him). But for almost seventy years which is called the minor occultation, he was in contact with his followers because he had determined four individuals, one after another as his special representatives with whom people met and through whom, they posed their religious and scientic questions and received answers.

But since 329, when his fourth special representative passed away, the major absence set in, and he did not appoint any other representative and referred people to jurists and great religious scholars to learn their religious edicts and teachings from them.

It is over 1000 years since the start of the major absence that the Shi'ahs have been looking forward to the emergence of the embodiment of divine justice and fairness who will put an end to the misfortunes of Muslims and direct them toward genuine Islam and felicity.

Of course, the anticipation of the arrival of the Imam of the age, does not mean that all Muslims and Shi'ahs remain idle and take no steps in advancing Islamic goals and merely wait for him but as noted scholars and Shi'ah scientists have said long ago, all Muslims and Shi'ahs are duty-bound to do their best for the prevalence and promulgation of Islamic rules and teaching under any circumstances and resist and struggle against oppression, tyranny, and wrongdoing, and exploit their resources to oppose them.

In other words, they should try to pave the way for the rule of justice and fairness, that is, they should train the society in a way that everyone demands justice and if oppression and injustice dominate the society, everyone protests against it and turns away from it. In short, every Muslim is obliged to sacrice for the cause of faith and Islam and be constantly ready to welcome the promised Mahdi ('a), that is, he should plan his life in a way that it is in accordance with that of the Imam, as to follow his line.

As it was noted earlier, the Imam of the age ('a) has been absent since 260 and the date of his reappearance is not known to anyone and if someone sets a date for his arrival, we are obliged to reject him.

Indeed, when oppression and injustice reach their height, when people are tired of tyranny and everyone demands genuine justice, that is, their mentalities have undergone a change, and when God deems it proper to send the twelfth Imam, he will reappear and the world will turn into a utopia and a heavenly garden.

Peoples' Duties During The Occultation

As it has been quoted from the Imam of the age ('a), during his occultation people are obliged to consult scholars and jurists and jurisprudents concerning their religious duties and affairs and obey their commands in every area of their lives. It is manifest that the great jurisprudents and scholars do not invent edicts and *fatwas* but they draw on the Qur'an, the Prophet's sayings, and those of the infallible Imams and present them to people and thus, consulting them is the same as consulting the Prophet and the Imams and the Qur'an and objection to them is like objection to the Qur'an and the Imam of the Age (look at lesson 30).

Is It Possible That Someone Might Live Over 1000 Years?

Researchers and scientists hold that the length or span of life is not the chief cause of death but it results from the disorders that beset one or all the organs of the body and so long as that has not occurred, the person won't die. If those disorders take place before old age and the natural length of life, the person will experience an early death, otherwise, death will typically seize us at old age. Therefore, if someone protects himself from such disorders, the length of age won't bring about death.

And the fact that at times, we read in newspapers and magazines that scientists are trying to nd a medicine through which to raise the body's aptitude for longevity conrms the point that mankind have the potential to live long but to do so he must work hard to overcome the obstacles.

Given this, if someone enjoys healthy and robust brain, heart, nerves, lungs, and stomach and knows all the hygienic precautions and takes them and knows the benets and harms of all the edible and the potable and utilizes them when necessary, it is not strange that he may live several times longer than typical people and even he might live thousands of years.

Of course, given the present conditions, not everyone can do so but considering the fact that the presence of such an individual (Imam) is indispensable, it is probable that God may arrange the system of creation and the chain of cause and effects in a way that he might take any precaution that is essential for longevity.

As we have already proved the necessity of the presence of the Imam of the Age with rational and quoted reasons, and also that it is possible for mankind to live a long life, if essential precautions are taken, and the fact that God can provide its necessary means for anyone He pleases, one can conclude that God, the Exalted, has supplied all the essential conditions for the Imam of the Age to prolong his lifetime. Therefore, this belief of the Shi'ahs, that the twelfth Imam was born in 255 or 256 and to this date (1392 AH concurrent with 1351 (AHS) that this book was written) and more than that up to the time that God wills, will have lived, does not provoke any natural or scientic objection.

Furthermore, even if his lifetime is not consistent with natural laws, God, the Exalted can keep someone young for thousands of years with His boundless power and through miraculous means. As the poet has written,

God that sustains the world
He will be able to keep a proof alive.

With a cursory examination of the Holy Qur'anic verses and the narrations of the infallible gures, one can prove the necessity and indispensability of a government at all times in the Islamic and Shi'ah school.

Islam has invited people toward gathering and contact with one another and the unity of stance and solidarity and has warned them against discord, division, seclusion and being a burden upon the society.

The Qur'an says,

"Indeed, the believers are brothers to one another" (The Holy

Quran, Surah al-Hujarat, 49:10).

"Everyone should clutch the divine rope and don't be dispersed" (The Holy Quran, Surah al-'Imran, 3:103).

It has been quoted from Imam as-Sadiq ('a), "Anyone who distances himself from the Muslim community even as far as a stone's throw, he has removed the string of Islam from his neck."[59]

Nahj al-Balaghah, sermon 127 reads, "Always stay with the massive congregations and the mass of people because the hand of God is with the congregation and avoid division. Truly, the man who strikes out on his own will be the prey of Satan."

From the aforementioned verses and similar ones, it is clearly demonstrated that Islam wants Muslims to coexist with unity and harmony and it is clear that to realize this goal, government and leadership of Imams is indispensable because they manage and organize the society and preserve the unity and solidarity of people and accurately run the social affairs.

It has been quoted from Imam Ridha ('a), "Indeed, the leadership of Imams is the guardian of the religion and the system of Muslims, and the interests and the dignity of the believers. It is a growing root and a fruitful and shady branch. The integrity of the daily prayers, *Zakat*, fasting, the *Hajj* pilgrimage, struggle, (*Jihad*), the collection of taxes and alms and the endorsement and implementation of the verdicts and rules and the safeguarding of borders and boundaries of Muslims are entrusted to Imams and are carried out by him."[60]

An excerpt of Nahj al-Balaghah reads, "The position of the leader of the affairs is like the position of the string of the rosary to its beads

---

[59] 'Usul al-Ka, vol. 1, p. 403.

[60] Al-Ka, vol. 1, p. 200.

that keeps them together. So when the string is broken its beads are scattered everywhere and they can't be collected again. "

It has been narrated from the Messenger of God (S), "Obey the one to whom God has entrusted the state of affairs because he organizes the Islamic rules."

Therefore, it is manifest that Islam possesses a government and leadership. Now, this question arises, are the points and objectives that have been raised in aforementioned verses and narrations and similar ones, conned to the time of the Prophet and the infallible Imams and God, the Exalted, is content with the suspension of His rules and commands during the absence of the Imam of the Age and then God does not desire the interests and the dignity of believers and the safeguard of borders and the removal of the threats of the foes?

I can denitely say that it is not conned to that period and all these objectives continue during the absence therefore, the formation of the government during the absence like when the Prophet or the infallible Imams were present is essential and necessary.

From the examination of verses and narrations, having drawn the conclusion that even during the absence of the Imam of the Age, there should be a government, we turn to this question that who should be placed at the top of this government and assume the leadership of Muslims?

With a little contemplation and carefulness, we will learn that the leader of Muslims should possess the following characteristics:

1. He must be wise.
2. He must be a professing Muslim and a faithful Shi'ah.
3. He must be just.
4. He must be competent enough to manage the affairs of the society and Muslims.
5. He should not suffer from vices such as ambition, greed, cupidity,

compromise and negligence in affairs.
6. He must be a jurisprudent, familiar with the Holy Qur'an, narrations, and Islamic teachings and jurisprudence.

Since the leader of Muslims must certainly possess these qualications, the eligible jurisprudent for the leadership during the absence of an infallible Imam has been introduced and appointed in the narrations of the infallible gures.

And thank God, that in our time, the late grand Ayatullah Imam Khomeini, who was one of the manifest embodiments of a qualied jurisprudent could demolish the monarchy and eliminate tyranny and oppression and exploitation with awe-inspiring diligence and perseverance and the help and the extensive efforts of the seminaries and the devout and faithful people and formed a government that was desired by the saints (Awliya') and assumed the leadership and brought Muslims and Shi'ahs the credit to enjoy an Islamic state which is based on the leadership and sovereignty of a qualied jurisprudent.

At the conclusion of this lesson, it is necessary to bear in mind that obedience to the sovereignty of the jurisprudent and the leader of Muslims is like compliance with the Imam of the Age ('a) obligatory and as it has been narrated from Imam as-Sadiq ('a), "Anyone who rejects the edict of a sovereign jurisprudent is like he has rejected an infallible Imam and the rejection of an infallible Imam constitutes indelity and apostasy."[61]

---

[61] 'Usul al-Ka, vol. 1, p. 67.

www.ingramcontent.com/pod-product-compliance
Lightning Source LLC
LaVergne TN
LVHW041616070526
838199LV00052B/3171